Give Fear A Knock Out Punch

Dr. Paul Cannings

I0098327

Biblical Strategies to Overcome Every Fear that Binds You

Lightning Source Inc. La Vergne, Tennessee

Give Fear a Knock-Out Punch
ISBN 978-0-9841337-1-0

Please send your comments and requests for information to the address below:

Power Walk Ministries
7350 West T.C. Jester Blvd.
Houston, TX 77088
Telephone (281) 260-7402
www.powerwalkministries.org

Printed in the United States of America.

Scripture quotations are from the New American Standard Bible (NASB), unless otherwise noted.

For more information concerning other products we offer including:

- "Biblical Answers For the 21st Century Church" ISBN 978-0-9779840-3-6
- "Vision to Ministry" ISBN 978-0-9779840-2-8
- "Jesus and Money" ISBN 978-0-9779840-4-6
- "Keeping Love Alive Series" for strengthening marriages or the "Leadership Training Series" for training leaders
- "Why Can't Mondays Be More Like Sundays" ISBN 978-0-615-22292-9

Visit our website at **www.powerwalkministries.org**

For more information about speaking engagements please contact us by telephone at (281) 260-7402.

Give Fear A Knock Out Punch

Dr. Paul Cannings

**Biblical Strategies to
Overcome Every
Fear
that Binds You**

Acknowledgments

Without question I would like to thank my wife, Everette, for her continual support of this ministry. I give her my deep gratitude for all her years of sacrifice and encouragement, which has allowed me to remain focused. She has blessed me in so many ways. I truly appreciate her love and concern. To my sons, Paul Jr. and Pierre and their wives, Tanisha and Monica, respectively: I am blessed to witness your love for the Lord and each other. When I see your families, my heart is strengthened and renewed. To our grandchildren, Paul III, and Natalia, two of my greatest joys in life. I praise the Lord for allowing my wife and I to experience such joy.

I also thank Gail O'Neal for all the work it takes to make so many things possible. Her tireless commitment to see the Lord's work make a difference in people's lives is truly a blessing. It is because of the staff at Living Word Fellowship Church serving the Lord faithfully that I am able find the time to make this material available.

Special thanks to Miriam Glover for her insight, hard work and commitment to see this book through to the end. She has edited this work, proofread through much material, and has helped the vision become a reality, as the Lord has ordained.

Special thanks also to Pastor Earl Lewis for his commitment to Power Walk Ministry. He has been a faithful board member and a committed servant of God. He has made many sacrifices for this ministry that has blessed this ministry to progress and it has not gone unnoticed.

I cannot help but thank God for calling me to serve Him. There have been many difficult days, but each experience has taught me more, has strengthened my resolve, and has caused me to fall more deeply in love with Him. Growing in my relationship with the Lord has been one of the most challenging life experiences I have had, but it has been the single greatest empowering journey of my life.

I thank God for calling me to pastor Living Word Fellowship Church. I thank Him because it has driven me to desire to learn more about the Lord, to draw closer and closer to Him so that I can be what He wants me to be for His people. I love the people the Lord has called for me to serve because of their desire to know Christ and to make Him known. We have shared a lot together as a church family and it has blessed us to experience God more deeply as we learn to trust Him more.

Last but not least, I thank God for Dr. Martin Hawkins. His encouragement, insight and commitment to our relationship has blessed and lifted me. I pray God's blessings on Southern Bible Institute, where he serves as President.

Give Fear a Knock Out Punch

Biblical Strategies to Overcome Every Fear that Binds You

Introduction

I have seen many believers make decisions as a result of fear. Most of these decisions have affected them negatively.

The idea to write this book came as a result of many years of counseling and talking with believers as they shared their life stories. I am the Senior Pastor of Living Word Fellowship Church in Houston and have served in various forms of full time ministry since graduating from Dallas Theological Seminary in 1985. As you can imagine, I have seen crises and conflicts erupt in people's lives and witnessed fear become an overwhelming obstacle.

Within my own life there have been experiences that have created tremendous moments of fear. I can easily recall standing at my son's bedside, praying for his very life. I remember talking with my wife as we were leaving the house for work one day, then turning around to see her fainting and falling to the floor. We had no idea if she would even make it through the week. This kind of fear dominated how I called on the Lord. During these times, His Word created a challenge to trust Him when common sense seemed to make more sense.

What amazed me throughout this study is that the challenge posed by fear and the decision to become "fear overcomers", is not limited to just a handful of believers. It is what has been in place from the time of Adam and Eve. Satan implicitly developed and used fear to manipulate Eve into a "catch 22" type situation. At first, he tells her that to eat the fruit of the garden and she would not die. Next, he says that if you do not eat this fruit you will not be like God (Genesis 3:3-5). So on one hand, she does not need to be afraid of dying and on the other hand, she can overcome God's fear that prevented her from eating the fruit. This kind of fear trap is stimulated by doubt.

It is this same kind of fear that caused Elijah, a great man of God, to run from Jezebel. He was not sure that God would protect him since he felt that he was the only one of the Lord's prophets left (I Kings 18:22). Elijah doubted God even after witnessing His power during his encounter with the prophets of Baal. Yet, as we know, fear can be a potent influence in the lives of believers. Even though each believer loves God, fear can cause them to hesitate or refrain from doing what God has instructed them to do. This is why Christ told the disciples, "Do not fear those who kill the body but are unable to kill the soul; but rather fear Him who is able to destroy both soul and body in hell" (Matthew 10:28; NASU).

When Christ reached out to Peter, in Luke 5:1-11, even before he became a follower, He said, "Do not fear, from now on you will be catching men" (v.11). Christ first charge was to address fear with Peter, the disciples, and throughout his ministry. Peter would later say, "*But even if you should suffer for the sake of righteousness, you are blessed. AND DO NOT FEAR THEIR INTIMIDATION, AND DO NOT BE TROUBLED, but sanctify Christ as Lord in your hearts, always **being** ready to make a defense to everyone who asks you to give an account for the hope that is in you, yet with gentleness and reverence*" (1 Peter 3:14-15; NASU; my emphasis added).

Paul writes, "*Finally, brethren, whatever is true, whatever is honorable, whatever is right, whatever is pure, whatever is lovely, whatever is of good repute, if there is any excellence and if anything worthy of praise, dwell on these things. The things you have learned and received and heard and seen in me, practice these things, and the God of peace will be with you*" (Philippians 4:8-9; NASU, my emphasis added).

I learned over the years that there is a fear that must remain at the forefront of each believer's lives. When reverential fear is nurtured, our entire walk with God is powerfully influenced for a productive experience of the Spirit of God in and through us.

A reverent fear of God leads to wisdom and knowledge (Proverbs 9:10), creating a place of refuge where a believer finds comfort and strength in the most difficult times of his life (Psalm 27:1). It is required in worship

(Hebrews 12:28-30; 1 Corinthians 11:28-32), and the focus it creates blesses God's people personally, in their family life, their children and blesses them with long life (Psalm 128). A reverent or respectful fear of God is not terror fear.

Terror fear is removed from the life of a believer when they commit to obey God and therefore get to know Him personally (1 John 2:5; 4:18). When a believer becomes fully committed to obeying God, he will do whatever God instructs him to do (for example, Job, Daniel, Joseph, etc.). So there is no need to fear God because they are too busy getting to know Him intimately (John 15:1-17).

Knowing God through knowledge, wisdom and obedience leads to discernment (Philippians 1:9-11; Hebrews 5:14). Discernment is an outgrowth of a believers close walk with God (Colossians 1:9-12). Life will now become powerful, meaningful and productive. As such, reverential fear is critical and terror fear must be overcome.

I have found the process of the daily battle to overcome fear an amazing experience. I pray you would take the time to read the verses provided in this book, contemplate on the principles and allow them to bless you as seek to grow and experience the work of the Holy Spirit in your life. *"So then, my beloved, just as you have always obeyed, not as in my presence only, but now much more in my* *absence, work out your salvation with fear and trembling; <u>for it is God who is at work in you, both to will and to work for His good pleasure.</u>"* (Philippians 2:12-13; NASU, my emphasis added)

Faith leads to a powerful experience with God and conquers fear in all its forms.

Release the Grip of Fear
-Chapter 1-

Acts 14:19-23, Luke 5:10-11, Hebrews 10:32-39

I have been involved in missions since I was seven years old and no matter where my family traveled, I have never been afraid. At the age of 12, I went to a Hindu village in a remote section of Guyana and as I was leaving, someone threw a bottle that hit me in the head. My brothers and sisters teased me, saying that they aimed for the largest target they could find. Yet, when I came home I was jumping for joy because I felt like I was beginning to suffer for Christ.

However, many years later, my son called me and said that he had finished his New Testament theology homework and that he wanted to review it together. I said, "Sure, come home and let's go over it." When I hung up, this overwhelming fear gripped me. You see, these lessons were preparing him for our next missionary trip to Africa. I had never felt a fear so gripping. It felt almost paralyzing and I had to walk slowly back to my study. As I sat, slumped in my chair, I kept asking myself what I was doing. How could I take my son on this trip and risk his life? The risks were everywhere, a random violent act or something as commonplace as contaminated drinking water. Just as the memories of being hit with the bottle rushed into view, I called my prayer partner and we began to pray. Fear is just that overwhelming and can stop you in your tracks.

Fear is also immobilizing and many times believers become weighed down by it. Maybe you are afraid of losing your job or you might be afraid to openly say you are a Christian because of what others think about your beliefs. There are some people that are afraid of the unknown, so they read the horoscope. Julius Caesar was a great emperor who could take on any battle. He was held in such high esteem that when he came back into Rome, people gathered palm leaves and flowers. Yet it has been reported that this mighty warrior would run and hide in the cellars at the slightest sound of thunder. If it began to rain and thunder on the battlefield, he would run from his men and hide because he could not stand the intimidating power of thunder.

A little boy was told by his mother that he was going to do a great job in the Easter play at church. The young boy had one speaking line: "It is I, be not afraid". The young boy practiced his line over and over again while standing in front of the mirror. On the day of his play, he took a peek from behind the curtain and saw all of the people in their seats. As his turn came, he got nervous and said, "It is me and I am scared". Even after rehearsing it time and time again, fear dominated him and he simply said what he felt.

Have you considered how powerful fear can be, if we allow it? Fear shapes our will to walk or not walk with God. Fear can make us stop our prayer life completely. Fear can hurt relationships. Fear can cause people not to come to church. It determines the quality, depth, commitment and drive of our intimacy with God. Fear can determine the level of spiritual growth or it can hold us prisoner and stagnant. It would determine if Paul after being stoned, nearly to death, would continue on and preach the gospel (Acts 14:19-23).

This one little emotion can be that damaging. Some of us try to spiritualize it. We say we are "waiting on the Lord". For many, it is only when we are truly afraid that we say genuine, heartfelt prayers. When Christ called Peter to the ministry, His first instruction was not to fear (Luke 5:10-11). Christ knew that He must address this issue before telling him anything else. We must analyze this fear and gain an understanding of why it's so influential in our lives.

Types of fear...

In the Bible, "fear" is often used when a person faces an issue in their life, and although they understand it, they develop "wholesome dread" towards it. "Wholesome dread" means they can find a logical reason as to why they should not act based off this fear. The fear we are discussing is different. As this fear takes control, a person feels more like running away and withdrawing because the possibility of failure is so real. It is not an issue of logic but rather it is an issue of the power of your emotions overriding your will to obey God. The Bible describes this kind of fear as a lack of confidence. Too many times we see examples in the Bible of people choosing to shrink back from doing what God has commanded them to do (Hebrews 10:32-39). For example, Elijah, the mighty prophet of God, ran a long distance away from Jezebel, a single young woman (I Kings 18:4-5; 19). Why do you think he ran? He understood how wicked this woman was and he saw the amount of power she had in his country and he believed that he was the only prophet of God still alive. Jezebel had killed the prophets. Based on a logical evaluation Elijah decided he needed to withdraw to a place he believed was safe.

The Bible also talks about another kind of fear, called terror fear. This is the fear we feel when we are in the middle of the highway and an eighteen wheeler is coming fast in midst of much rain. It is a deer in the headlights kind of fear. This stems from our emotions controlling us to the point of freezing us when we know we need to move.

There is another kind of fear called reverent fear. This is the type of fear desired by God. He requires us to respect Him and to honor Him (refer to the Lord's Prayer, Matthew 6:9-13). He views this as essential to worship

(Hebrews 12:28-29). This fear stimulates spiritual development (Proverbs 1:7; 10:9) and channels the believer's focus on to God. It leads to blessings and a powerful walk with God (Psalm 112).

We need to understand and address fear because it can affect our spiritual growth (Luke 8:14) and steal the opportunity to experience the joy, peace, self-control and the strength for long-suffering that comes from the fruit of the Spirit (Galatians 5:22-25). If terror fear or 'wholesome dread' overwhelms us, it can hinder us from accomplishing God's purpose for our lives (Joshua 1:5-9).

Bait on a hook...

The Bible warns us in Romans 8:15 that fear wins when a person decides to be a slave to their flesh. The flesh is like bait on a hook for a fish in water. The fish does not have to bite it but if it is hungry it will eat. It is the desire of the fish's desire or "flesh" (in a manner of speaking) that causes it to bite bait when it has food galore in the lake. It chooses to take the easy way out because the flesh wants immediate gratification. Paul views it as a lack of spiritual maturity that drives a person to constantly back away from doing the things he should (Galatians 5:16-21).

"Flesh" in the Bible does not just refer to the skin covering our bodies. It is a representation of our weaknesses and susceptibility to sin. Flesh is like a sponge drawing sin in. It is so weak that it does not matter the situation, sin is always surrounding us. For example, David was a man after God's own heart (Acts 13:22) yet he continued looking at Bathsheba bathing for so long that his flesh succumbed. You see, our flesh has a taste for sin; this is why the flesh does not automatically respond to the things of God (Romans 6:19).

Your flesh and mine has an appetite for sin. When you look at your own life, you can see this truth in your own children. Children often imitate and remember the things you do wrong. More often, you will have to discipline them to choose to do right; yet they seem to need no reminder on how to do wrong. The flesh seems to quickly pick it up because it has a taste for sin. This is a why a person that is a believer must obey Romans 6:12: "Therefore do not let sin reign in your mortal body that ye should obey its lusts."

The flesh is also connected to the mind. Consider this story: There was a man shipwrecked and he was the only survivor. He swam to the nearest island and was excited to be alive. He went searching to see if it was desolate and soon found evidence of others. His mind quickly assumed that these people were cannibals. He vowed that no matter what happens, he would hide from them because the natives will eat him. He went back to the broken remains of the ship and found a Bible. He stayed awake, reading and reading, until he fell on his knees and gave his life to Christ. He was now confident that someone would rescue him. One day, he walked by the beach and saw footprints. This was the first time he has ever seen footprints on his side of the island. Everything he read about cannibals came back to his mind and he became afraid and went to hide. Could he actually be hiding from the very people God has sent to save him?

If we don't make up our minds to fight against the drive and push of the flesh, then we will sin (Romans 6:15-18). Our flesh is susceptible to sin and if left unguarded, sin wins. This is why Paul tells us to fight in order to make sure that it does not reign.

Romans 8:12-13 says:

> "*So then brethren we are under obligation not to the flesh to live according to the flesh, for if we are living according to the flesh you must die, but if by the spirit you are putting to death the deeds of the body you will live.*"

The Bible says the anchor to move us is found in Romans 8:5: "*For those who are according to the flesh set their minds on the things of the flesh and those according to the spirit the things of the spirit*".

How do you handle intimidation?

There was a guy in high school who intimated all of us by bragging about how he could beat up everyone in the school. He would stand in the middle of the playground, staring us all down, challenging each of us to step to him. His presence created a war and he sought to stimulate a need for war just about every day. Every time I would see him, I remember thinking, "What should I do now?" Galatians 5:16 advises us to walk by the Spirit and *"you will not carry out the desire of the flesh, for the flesh sets its desires against the Spirit and the Spirit against the flesh"*. According to God's Word, there is a war going on within us that has nothing to do with Satan. Once we get saved, we become more conscious of our own wickedness. Paul says in Galatians 5:17: *"...and the Spirit against the flesh for these are in opposition to one another. So that you may not do the things that you please; but if you are led by the spirit, you will do the things that pleases God."*

There are some people who just love to fight. Do you know anyone like that? They enjoy tension, stress and arguments. This is the reason reality shows are successful. People want to see the drama of relationships falling apart and they relish the fighting and bickering. There are factions, dissensions, disputes, envying, and drunkenness. God said these negatives behaviors and attitudes will not bring blessings because the Holy

Spirit remains dormant. God warns *"... that those who practice such things shall not inherit the kingdom of God"* (Galatians 5:21). If you act this way or even encourage this behavior in others, then you will not get the blessings that the Holy Spirit has planted in your life. We must lean on the Spirit, to keep us strong, because at the end of the fussing and fighting, you will find that no one has won the argument and in fact, everybody has lost. To manage the war between the flesh and the Spirit, so that a believer walks in the Spirit, we must set our minds on spiritual things (Romans 8:5-9) and not things that are temporal (Colossians 3:1-2).

A clear illustration of misunderstanding and misapplying this concept is in Iraq. The militants of the country cry that they believe in God and they must fight for their holy city. They constantly scream, "We are going to kill you, shoot you and blow you up". I think, wasn't it Satan that came to steal, kill and destroy? How can you call this God?

Fear is the root behind this kind of hatred, causing war after war. Several times in the Bible we are encouraged to "stir up" the spirit within us (Ephesians 3:20). If you live by "the spirit you are putting to death the deeds of the body, you will live" (Romans 8:15). We have to decide to put the deeds of the flesh to death. In Colossians, God instructs us to put the old man to death and put on the new man. This is a decision we must make (Colossians 3:9-10). We make this decision by committing to study the scriptures and apply them in our day to day lives. (2 Peter 1:3-11) We are to set our minds on the things that are of the Spirit (Romans 8:6; Colossians 3:1-4). I understand that when there are difficult things going on in your life, it may not be easy to "set" your mind and not to give into the lusts of the flesh, but that is exactly why God has called us to stir it up.

Stir It UP!

The question then becomes, how do we get stirred up enough to walk in this commitment? Before we talk about how we can accomplish this, we have to address our minds. Motivation begins in our minds. We've already examined that our flesh is weak and struggling. Gaining control over the flesh will require us to have sincere faith, according to II Timothy 1. Faith, as defined in the Bible, is the substance of things hoped for and the evidence of things not seen. Faith comes by hearing the Word of God (Romans 10:17). Therefore, I must open up my life to hear the Word of God because the spirit is like fertile soil seeking the Word of God so that it takes root (Colossians 2:6-8). As a person becomes more receptive to God's teaching, he also becomes more sensitive to the Spirit. In I Peter, we learn to be like a baby who hungers for pure milk (I Peter 2:2). Peter said stir up the Spirit because He is a spirit of truth and is the helper of Christ.

Consider it this way; before you write a check, you have to deposit the money. Christ is saying things can't get going until we make some deposits (John 16:13; Romans 12:2). What is our deposit? We must have a desire to crack open the Bible and learn it. Paul told Timothy that he does not have the spirit of "timidity", which means cowardliness. In II Timothy 1:2, Paul encourages Timothy since he struggles with fear. Fear is not of God and is a sign of immaturity in faith. We must grow past the fear stage by allowing our minds to be renewed by the Word with a commitment to keep it through the most difficult times of our lives![1] Paul told Timothy, in the same book, to study the Word (II Timothy 2:15). He told him it will keep productive and effective by addressing everything he is experiencing as a result of his commitment to the Word (II Timothy 3:14-17). It is the anchor that holds a person when their emotions are powerfully being influenced by the circumstances they are experiencing.

The word for timidity occurs only here in the whole New Testament. The word pertains to a state of being afraid due to lack of courage, hence "cowardice" (NRSV). The interpretation of the phrase "a spirit of timidity" depends on how spirit is understood. Spirit is used in a variety of ways in the Bible. If Spirit here refers to the human spirit, that

---

[1] II Corinthians 10:3-6; John 15:1-10.

is, to the inner being of a person or the state in which a person finds himself or herself, then a spirit of timidity is another way of saying "a timid spirit." The whole clause can then be restructured as: "God did not make us timid" (Translator's New Testament - TNT), "God did not make us cowards" or "God did not give us a timid spirit." It is possible, however, to take Spirit here as referring to the Holy Spirit, so that the clause is stating that the Holy Spirit does not make one timid. Many commentaries in fact offer this opinion, but only a few translations make this information explicit.[2] Some translations make a distinction between the first and second occurrences of "spirit," with the second occurrence being identified with God's Spirit.[3] "God did not give us a spirit of timidity, but the Spirit of power and love and self control".

While all three are possible, the second of these options (man's spirit) seems to make better sense. As is often the case in these letters, a list of qualities or traits is given, starting with the negative and continuing on with the positive. Here the negative trait is timidity, and the positive traits are power, love, and self-control. Power, as it is used here, is not physical but refers to the spiritual strength that enables Christians to be

---

[2] TEV, French Common Language Version FRCL.

[3] New Jerusalem Bible.

victorious over adverse circumstances and to remain faithful to their Lord. Another way of saying this is "strength (en) in our hearts (or, minds)."[4]

Anxiety and fear, a deadly blend…

One of the causes of fear is anxiety. Christ says you have to counter this fear with prayer. Philippians 4:8-9 advises us to try to set your mind first on the principles of God, not on the issue and not on the problem. Begin by refocusing your attention to *"…whatever is true, honorable, right , loving of good repute, if there is anything excellent or worthy of praise let your mind live there."*

Again, we are not to allow our fears to detour us from being committed to obey God by faith.

God is always blessing us and always faithful to us. He never leaves us or forsakes us.[5] We can find ourselves, like Paul always giving thanks, even in the midst of trials and

---

[4] UBS Handbook Series. Copyright (c) 1961-1997, by United Bible Societies.

[5] Hebrews 13:5.

hardships. He says to set your mind and let it dwell and this will stir up the Spirit within.

Right before I left for my trip to Africa, my dad fell down and hurt his hip. I became nervous and agitated, wondering how I could leave my elderly parents while they are in need of my help. How can I handle all my obligations? I prayed asking God give me a break. Then I realized that He said do not grumble and complain (Philippians 2:14). So I began to thank God that my dad only had a broken hip and not a broken neck. I thanked God that he is in the reputable hospital with good health and insurance. I thought of the blessing of his wife. He was married to a godly woman who would stand by his side through thick and thin. I boarded my flight feeling assured that God is able to do "...exceedingly, abundantly above all that I could ever ask or think" (Ephesians 3:20). God says to dwell or think on these things and you will find yourself lifting Jesus up in spite of your trials and hardships. I refocused my attention from my problems and onto God's ability. **When our belief in our ability outweighs our trust in God's ability, fear wins.**

My youngest son gives a clear example of changing your mindset to align with a biblical viewpoint. One day when he was in college, he called to say that he was broke and doesn't have a clue how he will make it through the end of the semester. I simply reminded him of his blessings, namely, he has a lunch card that is pre-paid, so all he has to do is show it and he will eat. I told him to think about his dorm room and the comfort of having a place to stay. Think about the books that I paid for so that he could get a degree. Then I told him to stop thinking about not having money and how he can't afford to go on a date. Why not take the girl to the basketball game where you can use your lunch card? Take her to the cafeteria and sit by the trees. Obviously, none of this helped but he got the point. There was really nothing to complain about. He just lost focus.

Keep your eyes fixed...

The discipline we must all seek to develop is to keep our minds fixed on Christ as we live out His Word daily. This allows us to experience less fear and greater strength. The more we consistently obey God, the stronger His influence develops in us through the work of the Holy Spirit (John 14).

Wholesome dread makes you look at something and, based on common sense, decide not to press forward because the circumstances seem too difficult. Christ is saying that He can do a lot for us. But as long as we keep our eyes on our fears, then that same fear will keep our minds on the problem instead of the lesson He is teaching us Biblically (Hebrews 12:4-10). The issue becomes more about remaining committed to the Word of God allowing Christ to take us higher and do even greater things in our lives despite the issues before us (II Peter 1:3-11). This allows us to also work out our deliverance by having a reverent fear of Christ rather than a fear of the issues we are experiencing (Philippians 2:12-13). Christ said that He would lead you through the valley of the shadow of death because He is your rod and your staff. Even if you are hurting and you follow Him, He will comfort you. Even if you are broke, He will lay the table before you. Even, in the presence of all your enemies, Christ will let your cup run over (Psalm 23).

I have learned that if we don't release the grip of fear, we will not stir up the faith that is already within us (Romans 10:17).

"The fear of a man becomes a snare but whoever trust the Lord shall be safe" (Proverbs 29:25).

My son and I went to Africa, and by the grace of God came back safely. This experience and others has led him to commit to missions and is now our church's Youth and Missions Pastor.

Trust the Fear Terminator
-Chapter 2-

Isaiah 41:9-10; Psalm 115:11-15

But trusting God is hard...

When you were a child, you may have struggled with your fears. Fear of the dark may have prodded you to sleep with a night light. Perhaps you were afraid of being alone, especially the first time your parents allowed you to stay home all by yourself. Thoughts of monsters under your bed may have kept you tossing and turning all through the night.

Now, as adults, we may have replaced childhood fears with broader fears, such as family crisis, money problems, crime, global warming, job insecurity...and the list continues.

Fear and its companion, worry, sometimes seem to dominate our lives and our thoughts. I wonder what Jesus has to say about fear, an often paralyzing emotion.

As I searched through the scriptures, I found Jesus actually talked a lot about fear. In fact, He continually counseled us not to fear. As Jesus traveled throughout His ministry, fear oftentimes snared His disciples. One time, He commanded Peter to follow Him, and right in the middle of the walk, He turns to Peter and said "Don't fear" (Luke 5:10-11). They weren't even discussing fear! But Jesus knew Peter's heart. Look at Elijah the Prophet, who killed hundreds of false preachers in one day. Yet he ran in terror from one woman, Jezebel (1Kings19:3). Why? He was afraid. Consider Moses, God's chosen leader, who was afraid to step into his calling and lead the people out of Egypt.

Why is fear such an issue?

When God called us to salvation He had a plan for us. He did not just call us to gain the American dream of a house with a white picket fence and a nice car. Those things are wonderful to attain, but God has called each of us for a bigger mission. God wants us to replace the dream of personal wealth and focus us on the goal of a faith walk with Him. He is calling us for a purpose beyond just living a comfortable life of beautiful furnishings. There are things that He wants us to do, yet He knows that fear is holding us back.

Let's look at Peter, one of the more vocal disciples. Peter battled fear all the way to the cross. He was so conscious of the dangers Christ allowed them to experience that he traveled with a knife. When Jesus invited him to leave his routine life of fishing and follow Him, Peter did not really understand what was involved in this new life. This walk of discipleship training exposed Peter to scary and life threatening situations. He was caught twice in raging stormy seas: first, when Jesus was asleep on a boat (Matthew 8:23-27), and another time when Jesus told him to come to Him by walking on water (Matthew 14:22-33). The path to the crucifixion was often filled with dangers for the disciples.

Jesus warned Peter that fear would be an emotion that would negatively affect his walk with God. Fear removes faith and causes a believer to depend on their ability rather than God's ability. It was fear that caused Peter to deny Jesus three times (John 20:15-17). On several occasions Jesus reminds Peter to get rid of his fear – it was blocking his spiritual progress.

God values progress and He did not save us to be stagnant – we are **not** the same as we were before being redeemed. God came with a heavenly focus and plan and He promises to see this plan through completion. My life bears this truth out. When I decided to go into ministry full-time, I had many fears and concerns. I walked away from a successful job with health benefits, a retirement plan and possible promotions. I left it all to start a church. I remember questioning the future and struggling with the unknown. Would I be able to support my growing family? Emotions and doubts collided in my head until I realized they were rooted in fear. I woke up one morning and said out loud, "I choose not to let fear have the final word in my life".

We have no control over whether tomorrow is going to be good or bad. Why let what we cannot control dictate our life's path? Too many of us would rather live in what we can control today, than to trust that tomorrow will be better.

Every one of us must become "fear overcomers" – otherwise we would live more in fear than in faith. God rewards faith. In Hebrews 11:6, God says faith worships Him, pleases Him and He rewards those who exercise faith.

God does not bless us when we choose to live in fear. When fear has taken over, we isolate ourselves from other people and more importantly, from God. We take our focus off of Jesus Christ and have tunnel vision, solely seeing our circumstances. Our problem is now bigger than anything else in our world.

We experience this throughout our lives in a variety of situations: we let our bank accounts determine **if and how much** we will tithe, we allow circumstances to cause our commitment to Christ to falter, and slowly sin and disobedience enters our minds.

The Fear Terminator lives...

I really enjoyed the "Terminator", a movie about an alien robot sent to earth to protect a young boy by destroying the enemy determined to kill him. Let me tell you, the Terminator means business and when he shows up, people will be terminated. He is very powerful and operates without any emotion, especially fear. This allows him to take risks and face challenges head-on in order to complete his mission. When we act, fully trusting God and letting go of our fears, we become "terminators" of a sort, eliminating the enemy and gaining the victory.

Shortly after 9/11 occurred, I had to travel by plane to Africa for a short term mission trip. I said in my spirit that "I will not live in fear and that I will go where God sends me". Having encouraged myself, I boarded the plane with the other travelers. Already in his seat, a young man clearly of

Middle Eastern background sat reading the paper. As I walked past him, I could feel the atmosphere heavy with tension. On that day I was a witness to racism at its worst. Every move that young man made, he was followed. The flight attendant followed him to the restroom and even stood by the door. I too found myself staring and whispered in my heart,"Lord, if he was any other color I probably would not look at him. Forgive me." Fear does not respect anyone. Fear wants to stop us from being who God wants us to be. Fear triggers us to react on emotion, so we begin to see potential danger and problems everywhere.

Fear can drive us...

Fear can drive us to think about why we can't get something done, rather than focusing on what God says we must do.

In Isaiah 41:9-10, God tells us:

> *"You whom I have taken from the bottom of the earth, And called from the remotest parts of the earth*
> *And said to you, 'You are My servant,*
> *I have chosen you and not rejected you.*
> *Do not fear, for I am with you;*

*Do not anxiously look about
you, for I am your God.
I will strengthen you, surely I will
help you,
Surely I will uphold you with My
righteous right hand."*

God is focused on His record of works
and actions with us. God clearly sets
before us what He has done for us and
we simply cannot ignore the many
times He has shown us His love and
mercy. He saved us from the depths
and brought us into a loving
relationship with Him. If that record
cannot make us drop our fears and
begin to trust God, then what will?

God gives us examples of His saving
love for us. He describes his
relationship with Abraham and the
nation of Israel, explaining that Israel
was in slavery to Babylon for 70 years
because they chose not to obey His
holy practices. Even during this trying
time, God showed Israel mercy.
Notice, Israel suffered for only 70
years, not 100 years or even till the end
of time. God, in His mercy and grace,
limited the years to 70. The people of
Israel made the trip back to Jerusalem
safely, not because they had superior
weapons and giant cannons, but
because God provided protection and
direction. God moved King Cyrus to
release them and it was God who led

them home. It was God's covenant with Abraham that allowed them to still retain ownership of the land, even after all this time had passed, and it was He who protected them from all invaders.

God made this covenant with Abraham not because he was a nice guy that never sinned. Abraham struggled with fear. Let me explain: Abraham was married to the beautiful Sarah, the love of his life. He decided to go to Egypt because God allowed a famine on their land. Abraham knew that Pharaoh liked beautiful women. Despite the assurance from God that he was to be richly blessed and become the father of many nations, fear seeped in Abraham's heart. All Abraham could think of is the peril he would face if the powerful Pharaoh liked his wife. Intimidated, Abraham told his wife to lie and say she was his sister in order to save his own life.

When Pharaoh saw Sarah, he knew he desired her. Abraham allowed Sarah to leave him and join Pharaoh as his wife. Why would a husband allow his wife to be with another man? Fear, plain and simple. Since Sarah was such a beauty, Abraham figured it was just a matter of time before Pharaoh would come after him and kill him in order to make her his own. Fear can lead a man to make foolish decisions.

God chose Abraham and made a covenant relationship with him. Remember, Abraham was not seeking God, God chose him. Before we choose to accept Jesus into our lives, He had already died on Calvary's cross for our sins. In Romans 3:10-11, it says that no man seeks God; we were all running from God. It is God, according to John 6:44, who chose us, came into our hearts and drew us to Himself. It was God who gave us the faith to accept Him. Faith comes by hearing and hearing by the Word of God (Romans 10:17).

The only way that we can have the faith to say that we believe in Jesus is because He permitted the Word of God to permeate into our hearts. When we say "yes", God had already nailed His only begotten Son to Calvary's cross. There is no reason for Him to seek us and every reason for Him to walk away from us. Even when we try our best to do "good", our righteousness does not please Him. In fact, God compares our good works to filthy rags. God could have rejected us and let us go to Hell forever, yet by His love, He chose to bring us to the cross of salvation.

Does this unending love move you to trust His record? In how many more ways does He have to prove His love? When we are not seeking Him, He reaches out to us and provides us salvation that removes our past, present and future sins (Romans 10:9). Then He infuses us with the Holy Spirit (Romans 8:9-17). He also put angels around us (Hebrews 1:14). Apostle Paul says we live in heavenly realms (Ephesians 1:3). He did this because God so love the world, not because we so loved God. How could someone reach out to us that much and still have to convince us to trust Him and not fear?

Sometimes, I sit back and think of all God has arranged so that you and I would say yes to Jesus. He may have placed you with parents who walked with the Lord. If your parents did not have a close relationship with Jesus, then He allowed you to be employed alongside a Christian co-worker. Perhaps you were channel surfing and found a spiritual broadcast. Or you were on a business trip, and found yourself alone and lonely in the hotel room and you picked up the Gideon Bible. Others discover our Lord in the jailhouse. He did all of this so that one day we would say "Yes, Lord". He brought us to Himself and provided to us **7,000 thousand** promises in His Word. How can we say to God that we are fearful of doing what He says?

God is screaming out your name….

In Isaiah 41:9, the Lord said that He went to the ends of the earth for us: "I called from the remotest parts", the areas where no one wants to go. The word "called" means screaming loudly. God was specifically looking for us, calling out to us passionately. He knew who He wanted and who would come. He has a divine plan for us and that plan is to make us His servants. In verse 10, God tells us do not fear. Take note that His first words are an encouragement not to fear. His first instructions were not worship me, honor me or even obey me. "Do not" means we **must stop** immediately what is already set in motion. In other words, we sense fear and want to react out of fear, without taking the time to think. We cannot let fear control our thoughts, actions or decisions.

Many years ago, when we first opened the Christian Outreach building on our church campus, we held a leadership training workshop. One of the first group activities involved standing on a chair and falling back in the arms of your team members. I was a little uncomfortable with just falling and trusting, hoping, I would be caught….what if I fell? So, I came up with a slightly different plan, one where I would be in control. When my time came, I started asking questions, like "Do you go to the gym?" "How much can you bench press?" Then the workshop presenter said that I was next. But I still had more questions: "How big was the person that went before me?" If I was going to give up **my** control, I wanted to at least have confidence (control) in the persons assigned to catch me. Trust is the complete opposite. Trust requires you to let go of your control. When situations in our lives are out of control, we race around trying to manage everything until we get it back under control. Trust offers no safety net, so there is nothing to hold onto while you let go. You believe that everything will be cherished and protected in hands of the keeper. Isaiah 41:10 says, *"For I am thy God; I am able to preserve and strengthen thee."* The God of heaven was their God; and as He had all power, and that power was pledged for their protection, they had nothing to fear.[6]

This is the kind of trust that He desires. This is why God doesn't just want to tell us about His record, He would rather us learn about the person of Jesus Christ. Jesus will catch you when you finally let go and fall – it's in His arms that you will rest. Now, we can begin to understand (verse 10), the instruction

---

[6] Barnes' Notes, Electronic Database. Copyright (c) 1997 by Biblesoft.

not to fear. In that one verse, it's as if God is calming our fears by letting us know that He is Lord God and in need of nothing and will give you everything.

Remember when Moses said, "Who should I say sent me?" God answered, "I am that I am" (Exodus 3:13-14). When God takes over, the situation changes. Think of it like this, it's as if God said:

> If you need to open the Red Sea, put the stick over there. If you need the river Nile to turn into blood, just do this and it will turn.

God does not have to go and get blood from some place and pour it in the spot. If you need to get water out of the rock, and then speak to it, you don't have to hit it anymore. You can fight the war and none of your soldiers will die because "I am that I am". I sustain Myself by Myself and I continue all alone and I don't need help from anybody to be Myself.

Why can't we trust a person like this? With this kind of person we can be broke and He will still be the great "I am". I am not talking about the kind of broke where you have no ready cash but your retirement CD account is still available or where you have to transfer funds from one account to another. I mean you have no money in any account and have no means of getting any money quickly. Peanut butter and jelly is your breakfast, lunch and dinner. When we get this kind of broke, we need help. God understands us. That is why the words that follow "do not fear" is "I am".

You don't need to look about anxiously. God says I am with you and then He says I am God. Why would He do that? He did not say it in reverse, I am God and then I am with you.

God is very specific.

When He says I am with you that means, in the New Testament, the Holy Spirit is in us (Ephesians 3:16), He has angels around us (Hebrews 1:14; Psalm 34:7), Christ is our Intercessor (Hebrews 8:1-2) and walks with us when we are weak (Hebrews 4:16). Christ is not just in heaven watching over us, He is with us and in us (1 Corinthians 3:17). No matter where we go we are His temple, and He is every moment with us, therefore who can be against us when He is with us (Romans 8:31)? People may beat us down for a while but they cannot keep us down (1 John 4:4). God is saying don't worry about anything because when we are weak He will make us strong (Hebrews 4:16). This is why Paul says; "when I am weak, then I am strong." (2 Corinthians 12:10). As a result, the greatest need we have is to trust Him (Proverbs 3:5).

Many times God can't bless us because fear controls whether we act with the confidence and trust in Him. Do we remember that God is alive and in us at all times? We must behave as if we know and trust Him. *"For all who are being led by the Spirit of God, these are sons of God. For you have not received a spirit of slavery leading to fear again, but you have received a spirit of adoption as sons by which we cry out, Abba, Father."* (Romans 8:14-15).

Why do we pray less in the midst of trouble? Why do we miss church service? Why do we choose to believe the lie that we have to get things right before coming back? We wouldn't go to the doctor's office and say that I have to get healed before I can get examined. Do we really trust that He is what He says He is? We walk around on His planet, breathe His air, pump His gas and then tell Him that we cannot trust Him. If we don't trust God, why accept all His benefits? Whether or not we are ready to believe it, we are completely dependent on God.

Let's briefly examine two great men of the Bible, Peter and Daniel, and view their predicaments from a human perspective. When Jesus called Peter to walk on the water during a storm, I can imagine how Peter must have felt. It had to be daunting for a well-seasoned fisherman, like Peter, who had undoubtedly been through his fair share of storms and understood the deadly risks. The boat, probably not much more than a mere raft, was meant for fishing calm seas. What trust it must have taken for Peter to get out of the boat and right into the midst of the raging storm and walk on the water! He did it because Jesus was already walking on it. Jesus had already provided a long history with Peter of being the "I am". This record combined with Jesus himself walking on the water, worked with Peter's faith, so he could join the Lord. Peter knew and believed that God was with him in the midst of the storm. Peter started to sink as soon as he went back to looking through the eyes of a man. His weakness showed.

Daniel also exhibited great trust in the Lord when he refused to stop praying and worshipping the Lord, even if the consequences meant certain death. Daniel was committed to live for God and if that meant death, he would not back down. Every day Daniel went to the same window to pray knowing that his enemies were after him. Indeed his enemies found him there and trapped him. Daniel was then sentenced to be thrown into the lion's den, a certain death. God could have had the lions die the day before Daniel was thrown into their den. God could have changed the circumstances so that the king would not agree with Daniel's enemies, but none of this took place. Instead God allowed the lions to be hungry in the den with Daniel all night. I wonder how Daniel felt, staring into the mouth of a lion. The verse does not elaborate if the lions growled or moaned, simply that they did not eat him. How could Daniel be so confident in the face of death? Daniel understood his relationship with God. He recognized that he was vulnerable and weak all the time, and God was powerful all the time. So Daniel determined he could trust God **inside** the cave, just as he trusted Him **outside** the cave. Daniel knew that He is the same God outside as He is inside, whether you are in a cave or a big city. As Paul writes, *"I accept my weakness because He is strong"* (2 Corinthians 12:7-10).

When I rest in His arms, this is when I am strong. Faith comes to life when we recognize He is the "I am" and believe in His person. My mom is such a strong believer that when she prays at five o'clock every morning, she believes that God answers. In fact, she expects it. She believes in the power of God's Word. Since what she is praying for does not violate the Word of God, or is a direct promise in scripture, she expects God to answer. Mom believes God is going to do His will and since her request is in line with His Word, her needs will be met.

God invites and welcomes us to get to know Him as a person. If we understand who He is and trust what He says, then we can step out no matter the risk or the danger. Many times we don't think of God in this way. We see Him as a church building or even the Bible, and never take time to learn His character. Learning who He is as a person is crucial to loving and obeying Him. He is the Lord and has full authority and can fix whatever whenever He wants.

Psalms 115:12 says the Lord has been "mindful" of us. "Mindful" means He does not need us to remind Him that we exist. This great God is always thinking of us. He holds us so near to His heart that He knows the number of hairs on our head (Luke 12:7). His eyes are constantly upon us (1 Peter 3:10-12). "Upon" means His forehead is directly against ours, providing to us

His full attention. God does not have to be brought to where we are where we are because He is there, ready to respond.

On a recent missionary trip to Africa, I brought my mobile phone with me. I was concerned that using it so far from home would be complicated and challenging, I had my staff write down precise instructions. One day one of our mission leaders had to make an important call to the states. To my surprise, she got on and off the phone in a matter of minutes. I asked her if making the call was difficult. She said "not at all, choose a service and dial the number, just as if you were in America". It dawned on me that the phone was not working on radio waves but via a satellite which picks up any signal that has been programmed in the phone. Before I could make my call the satellite was already prepared because it is mindful of me for the call. God already knows what prayer request we will have and He is waiting on us with the answer. He is just waiting for us to believe in His person as directed by the Word of God.

The Path...

The first step in developing overcoming faith is to become a God fearer through believing and trusting in His Word.

Psalms 115:11 says '*You who fear the God, trust in the Lord; He is their help and their shield."*

Fearing God is not the same as a God fearer. God fearing does not mean quaking in your boots with terror in your heart. Rather, fear in the sense that gives honor and reverence.

In verse 13, God says, "*I will bless them*". Bless means I will prosper them and make them happy. Jesus Christ tells us, *"If you believe in My record and trust My person and do whatever I say"*, then He will make us prosperous and happy.

Remember the example of falling into the arms of the group? It is not until you fall and they catch you that you can relax and feel joy. As long as you are standing and waiting, the stress builds up because either you will fall back or quit and step down off the chair. You cannot stay on the chair and do nothing. As long as you are willing to trust, you will find happiness. Now, I ask you, will you let go, fall, and trust?

No matter your occupation or how many valuables you own, God will bless you when you choose to be a blessing by trusting Him. He says when we give our heart to Him, He promises to prosper us (Luke 12:22-34).

Some days I used to think how can people in the Bible accomplish so much? Now I see the answer. I have learned to stand in the chair and fall back because it is not I that lives but Christ that lives in me (Galatians 2:20). I have learned to trust Him and fear nothing. The progress that God has for us will never come until we terminate fear and allow faith to come alive. He promises to reward faith (Hebrews 11:6).

Fear that Liberates
-Chapter 3-

Proverbs 14:26-27; 19:23; 22:4

Why is fear an issue?

I have asked myself through the years, why would God continually tell us how to gain control of our fears? Why is fear such an issue? In the book of Deuteronomy, God tells His people not to fear the unknown rather fear Him.

It can become a little confusing on what to fear and what not to... how can you be sure you are right? Let me give you an example of unsubstantiated fear. Do you remember the millennium computer crash scare? Many retailers were in a state of panic as they announced that computers across the country were expected to crash on January 1, 2000. As fears mounted, the public began stocking up on canned food and bottled water. It seemed as if the entire nation was in alarm mode and nervous. We were constantly reacting out of fear for an event that never materialized. It was as if we forgot to hold onto the reverential fear of God, the creator of time and the universe.

Fear is not limited to just the US. I remember once when I was in Africa, Dr. Faustin Ntamushobora talked about the horrific events in Rwanda when fear took over the minds of his people. One tribe leader started telling his tribesmen that if they let the Tootsies (another tribe) continue to multiply and develop, then one day they will attack and take over the land. As a result of the ensuing fear and panic, 800,000 African people died at the hands of their neighbors. Fear is that powerful. Appropriate fear and respect for God somehow was lost and replaced with a negative word that a man put in the hearts of his people. His message of fear turned an entire nation to irrational panic.

Living in fear…

We live in a time where America is living in fear. People are so afraid that fear determines if and when they leave their homes. The Bible warns us to "be wise in these evil days" (Ephesians 5:15-16). Fear even dominates how we treat one another. Common courtesy is often forgotten as we act rudely because our fears are in control. We are in bondage to our fears. However, Godly fear liberates us.

God wants to ensure that Satan does not drive us to such negative fear, because we then become unproductive and stressed. For example, did you know gossip or slander begins with fear? One person thinks another meant this or that when they didn't. Proverbs teaches us how to live productively in our day to day lives, including developing a healthy fear of God. Verse 26 says: "in the fear of the Lord there is confidence." This does not mean that God wants us to be terrified of Him. Remember, He is a loving God that wants to provide an opportunity for us to grow and mature in Him. He is a just God that is not going to let us continue living a life of waste and futility. He is a God of grace and through fearing Him He wants us to remember that He is an awesome, powerful God. He desires us to have respect for who He is (Hebrews 12:28-29) and it is with this respect we worship Him.

Choose to honor...

I give Him honor for the power that He has.

I give Him honor for the majesty that He is.

I give Him honor that He is everywhere, all the time.

When we go in the bedroom God is there. When we sit quietly to process our day, God is there. This is the God that welcomes us because we live in His holy presence every day. I give Him respect because He is holy and righteous. Until a person becomes conscious of God, their life will be shaped by the world's view.

A reverent fearing of God also motivates us to worship. The fear of God motivates us to say, "God, I love you". When we honor God and respect Him, the fear of God naturally creates continual worship (Hebrews 12:28-29) because it reminds us of the awesomeness and greatness of Him. Unfortunately, sometimes people have to be shaken up, usually by a crisis, in order to worship.

When we allow God to be the center of our lives, fearing God will become our strength. This means that because I fear God I understand what He is doing for me and I am in constant worship of Him. The word strength means that He is our fortress. He is the one that builds a wall around us. "The angel of the Lord encamps around those who fear Him, and He delivers them" (Psalm 34:7; NIV). This fear causes us to remember His character and nature. Recalling who God really is gives us strength. Strength also means "fortification, stronghold, i.e., a place or structure which is a safe place to reside against attacks (Proverbs 10:15; 14:26; 18:11, 19; 21:22; Jeremiah 51:53; Ezekiel 24:21; Amos 3:11).[7] Someone came up to me after Bible study one evening and said, "Pastor, you are such a strong person." I said, "No, I am as fragile as anyone else. I simply seek to maintain respect, remembering who God is and give honor to Him. This encourages me to trust and know that God powerfully watches out for those who love Him."

---

[7]Swanson, J. 1997. *Dictionary of Biblical Languages with Semantic Domains: Hebrew (Old Testament)* (electronic ed.). Logos Research Systems, Inc.: Oak Harbor.

Do you see how this can free us? If you honestly and passionately seek to honor Him and live in righteous fear, He will put you where you need to be so the angels can keep encamping around you. They are going to mark the spot and you have to be there because it is attached to fearing God. Even if we are too weak and can't come, if we just fear Him then He will bring us back. This is how to gain the strength to worship God. It is not our strength but His strength that makes us overcomers.

Job illustrates this concept clearly. Although he was living his life honorably, the Lord suggested Satan test him. Job was a blameless and upright man that feared God. Satan questioned what he could do to Job since God planted a hedge of angels around him. Job feared God and stayed in His protection. Satan could not find a way to corrupt him. God knows Job's heart and is confident in telling Satan that His protection is not the reason why Job worships Him. In fact, God allows Satan to take away all of his blessings to see the truth of his heart. Satan took everything from Job except his life but how did Job react? Job arose, tore his robe, shaved his head and fell the ground and worshipped God (Job 20:1). He worshipped because he feared God. He held a respectful fear of God, knowing that he serves a righteous and just God. *"And to man He said, 'Behold, the fear of the Lord, that is wisdom; and to depart from evil is understanding'"* (Job 28:28; NASU).

As Job lost more and more of his blessings, Job's wife told him to curse God and notice what happens next. She died. Job found security because he feared God more than anything that could go wrong in his life. He feared God more than being hungry, and homeless.

Imagine going from a position of honor and respect at the city gates to a man who is now disrespected, laughed at and mocked. In Proverbs 14:26, God's children will have refuge even in the midst of storms. His children will find shelter and never have to worry. Our shelter is defined as security, safety, and peace and rest (Job 18:14; 31:24; Proverbs 14:26; Isaiah 32:18)[8]. I am not worried what anyone can do to me because I have complete trust in Him (Proverbs 14:26).

Fountain of Life...

While flying from Chicago, I sat in an aisle seat with a young boy and his mom sitting in front. After getting settled, his mom took a little nap. However, the little tyke was not sleepy and was rearing to go when he looked right at me with a little smirk on his face. Now I understood what was on his mind and what the smile on his face meant, but plane trips are my catch up time. I try to

---

[8]Swanson, J. 1997. *Dictionary of Biblical Languages with Semantic Domains : Hebrew (Old Testament)* (electronic ed.). Logos Research Systems, Inc.: Oak Harbor.

catch up on my reading or work on my laptop. As soon as I begin working, I look up and see him staring at me with his eyes twinkling, as if to say "I'm ready to play". Then he drops his toy. He tries to get my attention and when that failed, he began rocking the seat. I gave my best pastoral smile and hand him the toy. Sure enough, he drops it again. Here is the trick: if I pick up the toy he will drop it again and the cycle goes on and on. So I reached over, tapped his mamma and said he dropped the toy. His mama took it, looked at him and sat him down. He respected his mom so he listened but he really enjoyed his freedom too. With his mother at his side he felt safe, and because he respects her, he waited until she was asleep to play with confidence in his secure environment. If he was on his own, he would first look for his mom and if she did not respond he would probably cry and become afraid. He probably would run from everyone including me rather than try to play with me. His confidence was strong because he felt secure with his mother right there at his side.

God said "there is strong confidence, and His children will have refuge. The fear of the Lord is a fountain of life" (Proverbs 14:27). Our strong confidence in God should lead us to take refuge in Him this security in the midst of reverent respect of God frees us to experience His life powerfully developing in and through us. "The fear of the Lord leads to life, so that one may sleep satisfied untouched by evil" (Proverbs 19:23). This powerful development of life due to a reverent and respectful fear of God also extends to blessings. "The reward of humility and the fear of the Lord are riches, honor and life" (Proverbs 22:4).

God wants to give us an abundant quality of life. The Bible teaches us that when we fear God, appropriate and honorable fear, we can expect blessings (Proverbs 1:7; 24:3-5). One of these blessings is the promise of satisfied sleep. "Satisfied" means you can sleep, fully and restfully (Psalm 128). God says when you sleep, it will be like a baby because you know that God is encamped about you (Psalm 34:7). "Untouched by evil" means that God is watching every evil to ensure that it never touches (harm) you or me. God, Himself, is supervising what can and cannot come to us. God can give us a promotion while we are asleep by whispering our names in our boss's minds. Do you know how many diseases He has healed us from in our sleep? Even the smallest needs do not escape the sight of God. For example, if your car is running on empty, God allows us to find gas money, whether it's in the seat cushion or in a forgotten pants pocket. God will arrange the traffic in order for us to avoid a wreck. We are saved by His grace time and time again simply because we live with constant respect for who He is and we are sensitive to what He expects from us.

The Bible says an evil person is a person that is unconcerned about what God's views. God is saying He will keep us untouched from the person that means to harm us. If people are talking about us, God will provide security. God is going to make sure that if we fear Him that we will live powerfully and untouched. "O taste and see that the Lord is good; how blessed is the man who takes refuge in Him! O fear the Lord, you His saints; for to those who fear Him there is no want. The young lions do lack and suffer hunger; but they who seek the Lord shall not be in want of any good thing" (Psalm 34:8-10).

So what puts the breaks on our blessings? Pride stops the fear of God. We make pride into a major theological study but pride is not that deep. Pride is to live independently from God. Pride sounds like this: I know what God says but I am going to do it my way, even if my way is sinful and goes against the teachings of God (Job 31:24-28).

However, **grace does not abound for us to sin (Romans 6:1-2).** We can't invite God to forgive us because we choose to sin. We have to humbly confess that we respect His Holiness. A person exhibiting arrogant sin was stoned to death in the Old Testament. Jesus Christ was equal to God but even He said, "Thy will be done" (Luke 22:42). Although the people wanted to make Him a king, Jesus knew that He couldn't do it (John

6:15). His Father's will has to be done. That is humility in action.

Humility means that we are totally dependent on God to do what He is going to do. People can't tithe on a Sunday morning because of pride. They say I need my money and God can wait. God responds by letting us have our way and keep our money, however, He will put holes in our purses (Haggai 1:3-12). Slowly but surely you will see your life start to unravel until you are left turning back to God. Remember, God is God and we must live each day providing Him the respect and honor that is due Him. The more arrogant we become, the more powerful God will show Himself. You will break before He does, every time.

As a pastor, I have seen broken people healed and forget to give God thanks. In one particular circumstance, a young man got off his hospital bed and bragged about the skill of his doctor. It was not the doctor's skill, but God using the doctor, that healed him. Remember King Asa? He died because he placed more trust in physicians than in God. Despite his great achievements, he did not provide God the respect and honor due him and it cost him his life (II Chronicles 16:11-14). When King Asa relied on God and, respected Him for His power and authority, God blessed him. Philippians 2:1-5 instructs, *"If there is any encouragement in Christ, any constellation of love, fellowship of the spirit any affection and compassion, make my joy complete by being of the same mind, united in one spirit, intent on one purpose. Do nothing from selfishness or empty conceit but with humility of mind let each of you regard one another as more important that himself. Do not merely look out for your personal interests but all for the interest of others; have this attitude in yourself which also in Christ Jesus."*

Proverbs 22:4 teaches us, *"Humility and the fear of Lord will bring riches".* A dependent, trusting respectful and honorable attitude towards God leads to blessings. God says if we humbly worship Him in reverent fear, He will make us rich, respect and long life (Psalm 112; 128).

When I was young, I had a dog named Nippy. I worked hard to train Nippy to be mean, even placing raw meat in front of his nose so he would get angry trying to get it. You see, I wanted a mean dog in order to gain respect. I was tired of the bullies messing with me. In fact, Nippy was so mean that when I walked down the street with him at my side, people backed down. If any bullies tried to talk to me, Nippy would growl. They would say come back without him and we will show you something. I realize that this was not kind or loving but to tell the truth, I enjoyed it. The fear that Nippy inspired gave me instant respect and I felt I had gained the fountain of life because I could walk my dog and no one could touch me. Satan is like a roaring lion seeking whom he may devour and God is our protector, similar to Nippy. God tells us that we must keep a reverential respect for Him and understand that without Him, the bullies will beat us up. God encourages us to walk and talk with Him, rejoice with Him and we will not have to worry about Satan. We have the fountain of life as long as we stay close to Nippy. Even when Satan tears away at all the good things in our lives, causing stress and strain, God will keep Satan away. Fear God and He will liberate us.

> *"Humble yourselves, therefore, under God's mighty hand, that He may lift you up in due time. Cast all your anxiety on Him because He cares for you. Be self-controlled and alert. Your enemy the devil prowls around like a roaring lion looking for someone to devour. Resist him, standing firm in the faith, because you know that your brothers throughout the world are undergoing the same kind of sufferings. And the God of all grace, who called you to His eternal glory in Christ, after you have suffered a little while, will Himself restore you and make you strong, firm and steadfast. To Him be the power forever and ever. Amen".*
> I Peter 5:6-11; NIV

Overcoming fear while developing reverent fear of God leads to a powerful experience of Him working in and through us. It is this mindset that also blesses us (Psalm 112) and add days to your life. "The fear of the LORD leads to life, so that one may sleep satisfied, untouched by evil" (Proverbs 19:23; NASU). "The fear of man brings a snare, but he who trusts in the LORD will be exalted (Proverbs 29:25; NASU). "The fear of the LORD prolongs life, but the years of the wicked will be shortened" (Proverbs 10:27; NASU, my emphasis added).

Practice walking in the right fear of God each and every day.

A Fear That Finds Favor
-Chapter 4-

Psalms 112: 1-8

How did they do that?

There are many great Bible characters that inspire and motivate me, but not for the reasons you may think. Interestingly, I really don't admire these prophets and leaders as they walk in the glory of their victory. I admire them much more in their suffering. How they chose to handle their struggle, how they used their enormous courage when facing enormous odds leaves me asking, "How did they do that?"

What motivated Elijah to stand before the greatest prophets of his day and declare his God as all powerful? These prophets were the movers and shakers of his day. They were so popular that they influenced an entire nation to turn away from the true God to worship a false god. They rallied the top business leaders and the most respected rulers in their society to cut their bodies and gnash their teeth (I Kings 18:26-29) – all for a god that does not exist. It seemed that when they spoke, all of society listened (I Kings 18:20-21). In light of how intimidating these prophets were, what gave Elijah the courage to stand before them?

Elijah challenged the prophets to call on their god to bring fire to the kindling (I Kings 18:25-29). He stood confidently, even openly laughing in the face of the prophets and their false god, knowing that his God would bring the fire. But **how** did he know? There was no word from God that promised a fire. There was no confirmation from God that He would do as Elijah requested. Elijah simply believed in God. But I ask you, what would make a man believe that much? Let us examine this in various ways.

Let's consider the amazing faith of three young men:

Meshach, Shadrack and Abednego were put into hot burning oven for their faith The oven was so hot that the guards themselves were burned to a crisp while stoking the fire to temperatures of seven times hot (Daniel 3:22). What gave them the courage to not only face their destiny but to actually sit and relax in the fire?

Joseph's faith walk…is it yours?

No examination of a faith walk is complete without looking at the life of Joseph. Joseph was a man who lived to please God. Although not perfect, he held to God's standards and sought to do what God wanted him to do every day and in every situation. So when he was tossed into the well by his own brothers (Genesis 37:18-24) or when he was sold into slavery (Genesis

37:25-36) or when he landed up in jail, wrongly accused of rape by his master's wife, why didn't he become bitter towards God? Why did he sweep the jailhouse floor with a smile and a kind heart (Genesis 40:1-8)? Why was he at peace even as he passed out water to prisoners, even as prisoners who were jailed after him were released before him? What kept Joseph faithful to God through the many years of his imprisonment? What causes people, like Joseph, to be so committed in their faith walk?

Paul praises God even when…

How was Paul able to praise God while sitting under house arrest and forgotten by his family (Philippians 4:4-9)? He praised in spite of all the oppositions that he experienced. It was so bad that Paul had to write II Corinthians to defend his ministry. He was willing to sustain the assaults and brutalities because he chose to stand for the things of God. Paul is the type of person that, in spite of being shipwrecked, beaten, and bit by a snake, would stand in front of Felix, with failing eyesight and stand up for God.

Can you imagine what Paul must have felt? He was abandoned by his family and deserted by most of the preachers of his day. He was most likely chained to two guards all day long and fed like a wild animal, yet he writes, "Rejoice and again I say rejoice" (Philippians 4:4).

How could he advise us to "be anxious for nothing", knowing that his life could end at any time (Philippians 1:21-24)? It is this same Paul who writes, "I've learned to be content in whatever state I'm in", while bound and confined (Philippians 4:10-12).

Paul was a great scholar and a man who spoke nine languages, yet he arrived at the point in his life to say "for me to live as Christ to die is gain" (Philippians 1:21). What kind of faith drives Apostle Paul to write, "I can do all things..." when all his material possessions have been stripped of him as he waits for death in a jail cell (Philippians 4:13)? Paul was so focused on our Lord Jesus that he had to count the riches that his parents had acquired as lost, he had to count the respect that he had in the community as lost, and he had to consider all the comfort that his life as a Pharisee afforded him as lost (Philippians 3:2-8). Fear of his circumstances clearly did not control Paul.

However, fear can be a powerful emotion to drive us to do many things. When we are afraid of losing our jobs, we often arrive 20 minutes early every day. Even if we have a raging fever and sneeze continuously, if we feel in jeopardy of our jobs, many of us will still make it in to work.

For others, a fear of not having enough money to pay the bills will make us endure an intolerable boss. The fear of losing our employment is a mighty motivator.

If we could take that same fear and move it towards God, think of the things that we could become...think of the things we would be able to endure...think of the situations that we can face and overcome. This kind of healthy fear doesn't just liberate us, it strengthens us.

Fear of the Lord is a good thing...

As we begin, let's develop a clear definition of fear – what it isn't and then what it is. In Psalms 112:1, we learn the first thing about this fear that empowers your faith so that we live powerfully through difficult situations. "It is not enough to fear God, we must also love Him: fear will deter us from evil; love will lead us to obedience. And the more a man fears and loves God, the more obedient will he be; till at last he will delight greatly in the commandments of his Maker".[9]

This fear is not terror fear; God does not want us to be terrorized by Him. He is not a terrorist. For example, if you've ever visited the White House you will remember feeling an overwhelming sense of awe and even

---

[9] Adam Clarke's Commentary, Electronic Database. Copyright (c) 1996 by Biblesoft.

fear because we understand the power that the President wields. We know the powerful machinery that is behind the office of President of the USA. He is the leader of the free world and as such, we give him respect. We may not be afraid to talk to the President, but our fear makes us very conscious of what we say in his presence. Along the same lines, when we fear God it should be in reverence or respect (Hebrews 12:28-29).

This reverent fear is what leads to a desire to learn about God and to worship Him. Proverbs 1:7 says; "*the fear of the Lord is the beginning of knowledge; but fools despise wisdom and instruction.*" The same is found in Proverbs 9:10, "*The fear of the Lord is the beginning of wisdom, and the knowledge of the Holy One is understanding.*" Solomon said in Proverbs 10:27, "*The fear of the Lord prolongs life, but the years of the wicked will be shortened.*"

The fear of the Lord does not just lead to a productive walk with Him; it also leads to meaningful worship. In Hebrews 12:28-29, the writer states, "*Therefore, since we receive a kingdom which cannot be shaken, let us show gratitude, by which we may offer to God an acceptable service with reverence and awe; for our God is a consuming fire.*"

The key is to define what constitutes the true "fear of the Lord," which was termed "the beginning of wisdom" (Psalm 111:10). He who has this true "fear" delights not merely in the theory, but in the practice of the entire Lord's commandments (Psalm 111:2). Such fear is far from being a 'hard' service, but is the only "blessed" one we can accomplish (Jeremiah 32:39). Compare the Gospel commandments (1John 3:23-24; 5:3). True obedience is not task work, as formalists regard religion, but a "delight" (Psalm 1:2). Worldly delights, which made piety irksome, are supplanted by the newborn delight in and taste for the will and ways of God (Psalm 19:7, 10)[10].

Men like Elijah, Joseph and Paul were more fearful of God than they were of men. This led them to trust in God's Word rather than forsake it in difficult situations because of the fear that may have consumed their hearts. It is their confidence in God that has them believing, as Proverbs 11:3 states, *"The integrity of the upright will guide them, but the crookedness of the treacherous will destroy them."* They believed that it was just a matter of time before the wicked will suffer. Elijah knew that God will bless those who obey Him and curse those who disobey Him. Elijah trusted God before the prophets of Baal (Deuteronomy 11:27-28). The Word of God is powerful (Hebrews 12:4), and does not return empty, *"So shall My Word be that goes forth from My mouth; It shall not return to Me void, But it shall accomplish what I*

---

[10] Jamieson, Fausset, and Brown Commentary, Electronic Database. Copyright (c) 1997 by Biblesoft.

please, And it shall prosper in the thing for which I sent it" (Isaiah 55:11, NKJV, my emphasis added).

Therefore, a man who fears God is blessed, meaning he prospers, he is happy and his household does well (Psalm 112:2-8).

It is not what we face in this life that matters most. It is our reaction to these trying issues. Are we filled with worry and fearful of our circumstances or has the issue stimulated a reverent fear of God? When Joseph was challenged by Potiphar's wife, he decided that he feared God more than the power of his master (Genesis 39:9).

There is no way to escape God...

You see, there is simply no way to escape God. In America, our culture teaches us that once we get a job we can prosper. It promises that once we get an education and have built a resume full of progressive job experiences, we can then negotiate for the salary our heart desires. Our culture tells us that when we have a savings account, health insurance and life insurance that we are basically secured. Our culture does not tell us that there is no amount of medical coverage that will take cancer out of your body. Our culture does not tell us that it is God that is the great healer. In fact, our culture encourages us to live independently from God. If we think that God is active and moving for our good in our lives, then we will

want to follow Him, learn His ways and apply His wisdom in our day to day living (Proverbs 3:4-6). It is this kind of reverent fear and love that increases faith overpowering our desire to live in fear.

The mindset of feeling independent of God reflects a lack of fear of God. Let's look at it this way: your husband is driving you crazy. You say to yourself that it's time you do what you want and find some happiness. After all, how long are you to respect someone who continually acts crazy? By your actions you are telling God, "Hey I don't fear you". Our actions suggest that our circumstances overwhelm our need to obey God.

We are told by the psalmist to "greatly delight" in God's commands (Psalm 119:35, 47). We are encouraged to be like David, passionate about the Word of God. In the midst of overwhelmingly difficult circumstances no one has to remind David to apply God's Word (Psalm 1). He is passionate because he is fearful of God; he has studied the character and record of God. David would say, "I can't wait to get into the house of God" (Psalm 55:14). How many of us greet Sunday morning like this? Or do we say, "I know I need to go to church but the kids don't want to go. Can we just skip it?"

> *"Though a host encamp against me, My heart will not fear; Though war arise against me, In spite of this I shall be confident. One*

thing I have asked from the LORD, that I shall seek: That I may dwell in the house of the LORD all the days of my life, To behold the beauty of the LORD. And to meditate in His temple. For in the day of trouble He will conceal me in His tabernacle; In the secret place of His tent He will hide me; He will lift me up on a rock. And now my head will be lifted up above my enemies around me, And I will offer in His tent sacrifices with shouts of joy; I will sing, yes, I will sing praises to the LORD."

Psalm 27:3-6; NASU

David was excited about God and he passionately desired to obey God rather than allow his circumstances to distract him from God. Do you remember when Hurricane IKE was encroaching upon Houston? Everyone in the city passionately looked at the weather report. In my opinion, we had the best news coverage with the largest listening audience ever. Even the reporters were delightfully passionate about the weather. If we can be passionate about the effects of God, why can't we be passionate about the experience and the person of Christ?

What is the point of being excited about the grocery store and never buy groceries? What is the point of being excited about your car and never drive it? What is the point if we live life but never look to the Maker of life?

The man who fears God is a man that wants to learn about God and wants to passionately pursue God and His laws. His very action proves his reverent worship of God. If we are not living in appropriate fear of God, then external fears will immobilize us and lead us to do things that will violate God's Word. Which type of fear will you choose?

External fears move us away from God. If Daniel didn't have reverential fear of God, he would not have refused the best food of Babylon and refuse to stop praying to God knowing the alternative is a lions' den. He would have worshipped the idol, like all the other Jewish boys, because he feared receiving the punishment of a very powerful king. Daniel obeyed God's law and was not afraid to walk in the truth. But the other boys were afraid of the king, who was simply a man (Daniel 1:8-16). They were so afraid that they ate the king's food and worshipped him while Daniel and his friends chose God's way. The person who fears God will become passionate about living out the truths found in the Bible.

Again this is not a terror fear of God. Terror fear does not build relationships. When my kids were young, I disciplined them. My kids were never terrorized by me, but I wanted them to learn that when I spanked them that it was justice. So they learned to respect me. When I spanked, it was because the choices and actions they made were wrong and needed to be corrected. I corrected it because God tells me that I have to or else I don't love them His way. Discipline, the Lord's way, is a good thing. I may fear that they may hate me for it, or never forgive me and the friendship I want with them maybe lost. But I must discipline them God's way and trust God for the results He promised. This is because my respect for God (reverent fear) is greater than the fear of not having a friendship with my children later.

Knowing right and choosing wrong…

To know what to do and not do it is sin. My dad was the type of person that when he gave you chores, he allowed no room for excuses. He said, "I brought the broom, the house and every cleaning product you need for you to get this house spotless." He would also say, "I could make you get down on your hands and knees to scrub but I have given you a mop and a bucket. So how can you tell me that you can't get it done? Haven't I also fed you? So don't you have the energy to do the chore?"

Sure enough, when dad arrived home from work, we had to have the house ready. All eight of his children would line up to wait our turn to show him what we accomplished. You see, daddy did not allow questions, explanations or excuses. His belt was all the reinforcement his words needed. Now mind you, dad also kept to his word. He had a rule that once we finished showing him our completed chore, he would not bother us in our play time. The minute he said everything was fine all eight of us scattered. This is the same father we came to talk to when we needed his advice.

Hasn't God given us everything that we have and own? Why would He take our excuses? Why should He? He said in His Word that if we abide in Him and *"My words abide in you ask whatever you wish and I will grant it"* (John 15:7). "Wish" means whatever you desire. The word "done" means I will create it just for you. This blessing will have your signature on it and it will be designed just for you. He says even if it's not in your town, He will create it in heaven, and put it in place for you. He would do all this because we choose to desire Him. We can't "abide" until we begin to fear Him. Once we fear Him, we will then reverence Him. When we reverence Him we abide with Him. As we abide with Him whether in good times or bad He blesses us with what we wish, creating it just for us.

Overcoming suffering is a recurring theme in God's Word (John 16:33; Romans 8:18; James 1:2-4). Joseph, Daniel and Paul mastered this process. I want to learn how to suffer and not allow it to destroy my commitment to God. I would rather these trials make me better not bitter. I remember as a teenager, I loved to play soccer. I was always on the field practicing, often for hours and hours. While running and leaping and scoring, I never felt hurt or pain. But once I hit the showers, everything I did on the field hit me; it seemed like every part of my body ached and was sore. Even waking up the next morning I would feel like agony- we would call this pain "coming to life."

Strangely though, the aches and pain never overshadowed the pride I would feel when looking at the field and knowing I gave it my all. I did things I didn't even know I could do. The Bible says when you walk with God you will do things you didn't even know you could. The Spirit of God is doing it in and through you. *"For this reason also, since the day we heard of it, we have not ceased to pray for you and to ask that you may be filled with the knowledge of His will in all spiritual wisdom and understanding, so that you will walk in a manner worthy of the Lord, to please Him in all respects, bearing fruit in every good work and increasing in the knowledge of God; strengthened with all power, according to His glorious might, for the attaining of all steadfastness and patience; joyously giving thanks to the Father, who has qualified us to share in the inheritance of the saints in Light"* (Colossians 1:9-12; NASU). The same is explained in 2 Peter 1:3-4 because we experience the 'divine nature' of God.

The Bible says when you abide in Him, then His spirit takes over and you can do much. God says, "My desire is your desire and what I am thinking you are thinking" (John 15:1-5). This is why a person who fears God is blessed. *"Praise the LORD. Blessed is the man who fears the LORD, who finds great delight in his commands"* (Ps 112:1; NIV).

Blessings of fearing God...

I would rather bless God so that I could gain a blessing. The only way to bless God is to do what He says to do because we fear Him. Psalm 112:2 says His descendents will be mighty on earth. His kids will rise up and be respected, have better jobs. He says the generation of the upright will be blessed. The people who walk with them that love God will be blessed from being around them. It says wealth and riches in His house and His righteousness, people will remember you forever. They will die and go to heaven and say God where is that person that did this for me. It is hard to hold on to something when God is not preserving it.

I recall once when I bought a car and did not take the time to pray about it. I had a hard time keeping it. Eventually I ended up asking, "Lord, help me to get rid of what I thought was a blessing that is not your blessing".

Proverbs 24:3 says:

"By wisdom a house is built, by understanding it is established, by knowledge the rooms are filled with all precious and pleasant riches; a wise man is strong and a man of knowledge increases in power."

Godly fear strengthens. Godly fear reduces stress. People all over the world are trying to reduce stress in all kinds of ways. When the Word of God shines on you, you will see in the darkness and those stressful behaviors, actions and people will be brought into the light.

Review John 1:5-7; 2 Peter 1:3-10:

"This is the message we have heard from Him and announce to you, that God is Light, and in Him there is no darkness at all. If we say that we have fellowship with Him and yet walk in the darkness, we lie and do not practice the truth; but if we walk in the Light as He Himself is in the Light, we have fellowship with one another, and the blood of Jesus His Son cleanses us from all sin."

When the lights get turned "on", we can do anything. When David's light is on, he can stand, unafraid, in front of Goliath" (I Samuel 17:26). His fear was controlled by his commitment to trust God's Word. The other people are stressed out and can't fight for 40 days (I Samuel 1:24); David enters the scene and says lets fight this moment (I Samuel

17:26-27). Why were the disciples on the boat so stressed out? They had placed Jesus in a box, limited by what they thought He could and could not do; so much so that when He walked on water they called Him a ghost (Matthew 14:22-27). Do you limit Jesus?

When the lights are out stress will mount. We must keep the lights "on" by fixing our eyes on Christ, who is the "author and finisher of our race" (Hebrews 12:2).

II Peter 1 greets us with a prayer of grace and peace to be multiplied unto us in the knowledge of God. If you want to experience this phenomenal grace and peace, then let the spirit of God open up your mind to see.

Only when I view life through the telescope of the true knowledge of God then will I go in the right direction. Otherwise, I would keep walking blindly. The more blind I am, the more walls I walk into and the greater my stress. True seeing comes from the knowledge of God, not the knowledge gained from random learning. If you have a fear of God, it will drive you to a knowledge that will open our eyes. We can then deal with anything in life because we understand that He has given us everything pertaining to life and godliness (II Peter 1:3-4). God says you will never stumble (II Peter 1:10). Stumble means to mess up so badly that you can't get off the ground. You will always be able to dust off and come back. This is not a sin here or a sin there; this is a fall flat on your face disgrace. In order to avoid this fall, you are to think on everything that is biblically based (Colossians 3:1-4). The minute you drop your guard, and stop meditating on the Word of God, you have let Satan step inside (Ephesians 4:17-24). The only way to keep Satan away is to live and speak the truth of God (John 8:44; 14:6).

In the midst of a difficult time in Timothy's life, a time when Timothy was fearful (II Timothy 1:7) of all that was taking place around him (II Timothy 2:14-26; 3:1-13), he wanted to resign from the ministry. Paul said to Timothy, *"You, however, continue in the things you have learned and become convinced of, knowing from whom you have learn them, and that from childhood you have known the sacred writing which are able to give you the wisdom that leads to salvation through faith which is in Christ Jesus"* (II Timothy 3:14-15).

Fear is a true natural human feeling. Overwhelming situations can quickly drive us to function based on our survival instincts. We must focus more on a reverent fear of God because this protects us, strengthens us and blesses us. *"Taste and see that the LORD is good; blessed is the man who takes refuge in Him. Fear the LORD, you His saints, for those who fear Him lack nothing"* (Psalm 34:8-9; NIV). People like Joseph, Daniel and Paul had a reverent fear of God that kept them God conscious and out of this constant experience and respect for God's holiness and grace they remained focus, committed to His Word and His promises and as a result experienced the victory they already had. A reverent fear of God creates an inner motivation that leads to a high level of respect for who God is which in turn leads to a sincere trust in God.

Victory over difficult situations is not something we create it is something we allow when we trust God's faithfulness. In Psalm 112:1-8 this fear blesses the life of a believer equipping them to deal with daily challenges.

The Traits of True Faith
-Chapter 5-

Hebrews 11:24-28

If God were to appear before you right now to redirect your life, how would you respond? Would the fear of uncertainty cause you to remain stagnant, staying in your comfort zone?

What if the life He is leading you to experience comes with a lot of pain and suffering? How would you respond to Him? When Jesus handpicked His disciples, it would seem reasonable to assume that their lives would be full of chariot rides, cushiony beds and abundant food? Peter's life was full of trials, constant whippings and he traveled so much that he never knew if or where he could lay his head for the night.

Let's look at Paul's life. Paul was a man who knew people in prominent places; he was a scholar, trained by the Pharisees and learned Hebrew (Philippians 3:4-6). He knew nine languages and was well respected in his day. One day on the road to Damascus, Jesus met Paul and decided to redirect his life. Paul's new path led him to many life threatening situations, including being shipwrecked three times and bitten by a venomous snake. He was beaten more times than we can count, stoned and left outside of a city to die. His family ostracized him, having nothing more to do with him.

They treated him as if he simply did not exist. He was shackled in a prison cell with no way to get out. Demas, a fellow believer, turned his back on Paul and began to speak evil against him because he did not agree with Paul's faith walk (II Timothy 4:9).

In Philippians, the preachers spoke against Paul, wondering out loud to any and everyone, if Paul truly was for Christ then why were all of these bad things happening to him? Paul said that some preach for envy, some for strife but as long as they preach Jesus Christ it is okay (Philippians 1:15-18). Paul was attacked so much that he had to write II Corinthians to defend his ministry. He was called a thief but Paul kept pressing because Jesus gave him specific instructions on the road to Damascus.

Paul's focus was clear. If Jesus were to give us a different call for our lives, would we obey or would the fear of uncertainty cause us to reject Him? If this calling challenges you to redirect your life, would you accept what Christ has to say?

Remember the story of Moses' birth and how he was rescued by Pharaoh's daughter, who in turn hired his mother to nurse him. His mom was always behind the scenes teaching her son the Jewish ways. He was given the best that life offers and he lacked nothing. He could have been content to live his life as Pharaoh's son and truly believe everything they thought him (Acts 7:22-25).

But his mother kept teaching him about Abraham, Isaac and Jacob. Moses had learned from the best Egyptian scholars, and had servants to make his bed, cook his meals and tailor his clothes. Moses' lived a story book life.

When Moses made up his mind to follow God, he leaves Egypt with absolutely nothing. Moses could have the finest clothes and just about anything else he wanted. Yet as he approached the age of 40, he decided to visit his brethren. He was soon to be inducted as a Pharaoh, meaning if he did not decide his future they were going to decide it for him. *"By faith Moses, when he had grown up, refused to be called the son of Pharaoh's daughter."* (Hebrews 11:24).

When God met Moses, through the teachings of his mother (Exodus 2:8-9), his faith had grown so much that it determined his purpose. Anytime you walk with God He will determine your purpose (Philippians 2:12-13). *"Therefore, since we have so great a cloud of witnesses surrounding us, let us also lay aside every encumbrance and the sin which so easily entangles us, and let us run with endurance the race that is set before us, fixing our eyes on Jesus, the author and perfecter of faith, who for the joy set before Him endured the cross, despising the shame, and has sat down at the right hand of the throne of God"* (Hebrews 12:1-2; NASU).

The minute we decide to walk with God, we no longer have any rights over our purpose. *"For you have been bought with a price: therefore glorify God in your body"* (NASU; I Corinthians 6:20). We cannot hold on to our way and expect God to follow our direction. St. Augustine said, "If you believe what you like in the gospel and reject what you don't like, it is not the gospel you believe, but you believe in yourself." In other words, you believe in eating therefore at the buffet you pick what you want. It is not because you believe in the chef but in your appetite.

In Hebrews 11:24 we find that Moses has "grown up", meaning he has completed all the preparation the Egyptians required to prove his readiness to manage his royal responsibilities. It is at this point that Moses was faced with a dilemma. Should he choose to be in Pharaoh's kingdom or become a part of what God has promised to do for His people? Moses' mother's teachings influenced him greatly and his choice was clear when he decided to defend a slave rather than join Pharaoh's kingdom.

This decision removed Moses from all the riches of Egypt and he accepted his new job, a lowly, dirty sheepherder. Moses followed God, *"choosing rather to endure ill-treatment with the people of God than to enjoy the passing pleasures of sin"* (Hebrews 11:25).

The Bible has worked out your purpose and we are told to run the race that is set before us (Hebrews 12:1). God does not say run the race that I am still in the process of figuring out. Before we were born, God already decided if we were going to be male or female. If the person does not have the gift of celibacy then it is set that this person has to marry. God says if we seek Him first He will give us what we need. We work at our specific jobs, so that we have opportunities to share the gospel and fulfill our command to be the salt and light. God wants us working so that the unsaved can witness first-hand how followers of Christ act, on good days and bad days. Some of our co-workers may not attend church yet they may have the opportunity to see church happening in the market place (Colossians 3:22-25). According to II Peter 1:3, *"...seeing that His divine power has granted to us everything pertaining to life and godliness, through the true knowledge of Him who call us by His own glory and excellence".* When you have forgotten your purpose then you no longer walk by faith. He gives us purpose when we go to the grocery stores and He directs us to feed the hungry. He expects us to buy food with His purpose in mind (Luke 4:17-20). Today, many people live "purposeless" because we have allowed the world to shape our purpose and define us. If your life today does not line up with the purposes of God, then we are saying we live a life that is conforming to the world's standards. *"And do not be conformed to this world, but be transformed by the renewing of your mind, so that you may prove what the will of God is, that which is good and acceptable and perfect."* (Romans 12:2)

In what ways are you following the world? Let's look: when we tell our kids they are grown at 18; when we cheer our kids at sports activities and not bring them to church. We should be as happy about our kids singing in the choir or serving God at a young age as we are when they get an "A" in math. We cannot allow ourselves to be controlled by the world's values or ways of thinking. It will corrupt us.

Moses clearly understood that his decision meant that he chose "to endure ill-treatment with the people of God than to enjoy the passing pleasures of sin" (Hebrews 11:25). If this were you, what would you choose?

Consider this: As a single young lady, you finally meet a man that has a job and a level of education. He is not Denzel Washington - but close. You find out that he does not have a relationship with Christ. Do you choose walking with God because He said you should only date someone that is saved (II Corinthians 6:14)? God's standard is that you date someone that is committed to walk with Him. Do you go out on Valentine's Day with him or stay home alone and light your own candles? This is when we have to decide that God shapes our purpose.

This dilemma is the experience of anyone you may name in the Bible, even Rahab (Joshua 2). After the death and resurrection of Christ, does Peter go back to fishing or does he become a fisher of men? Jesus never promised Peter a paycheck, status or power He just told him to go (Matthew 28:19-20; Acts 1:8). Christ told Paul to go to the Gentiles knowing the difficulty he would experience, yet Paul remained faithful (2 Corinthians 4:7-12). So why would Paul go out into this hardship, day after day? Because, despite the uncertainty that fear can create, Paul chose to obey God and live out God's purpose for his life.

According to Exodus 2:14, "*Then Moses was afraid and said 'Surely the matter has become known.*" It seems like a contradiction to Hebrews 11:27; *"By faith he left Egypt, not fearing the wrath of the king; for endured, as seeing Him who is unseen."* When Moses' faith (he trusted the information provided to him by his mother; Romans 10:17) is compared with his decision to leave Egypt, fear is displaced.

The verse in Exodus does not say that Moses feared the king. When it speaks of Moses' fear, it does so in the context of the Israelites knowing that he had killed the Egyptian. So his decision to leave Egypt was more about accepting God's purposes for Israel than the temporary joy of a great position. Even though Moses could not see, at the time, all that God would do, he chose to look towards God's future for Israel than his future in the kingdom of Pharaoh. This is an act of faith towards God than fear of a king.

The fear discussed in Exodus is the kind of fear to run, not as if you are quaking in your boots, immobilized. This type of fear, feeling the need to draw back and go another way, is called dreadful fear. For example, a woman who says yes to marriage but later changes her mind on her wedding day is experiencing uncertainty fear. The bride to be feels like withdrawing, as in not going forward.

Once we have made up our minds to obey God then we must put fear behind us and set our hearts for the long haul. Faith must be tied to endurance. Fear means I am relying on my ability to get it done. Faith means I am totally relying on God to fulfill His Word (Romans 10:17). God does not mind us talking to Him and telling Him all that is going on as long as we continue to walk in faith (Habakkuk). Faith means I will endure whatever comes because I have chosen to walk with God. Endurance means to "bear up" under the pressure of whatever God says to do. You can't walk by faith and complain every step of the way. We have to say, "Since this is the way I am supposed to go, I will take the drama because God's trials are better than anything else that I can ever experience."

Paul says to young Timothy who wanted to quit his leadership role in the church of Ephesus. Paul encouraged him, saying, *"Fight **the** good fight of faith; take hold of the eternal life to which you were called, and you made a good confession in the presence of many witnesses"* (I Timothy 6:12).

If a person is going to walk by faith and their actions are now under the direction of faith, they must commit to endure. They cannot expect an easy, perfect world because they have joined forces with God when the enemy is loose (1 John 5:19). Remember, the Bible tells us that the fruit of the spirit is longsuffering.

I Peter 3:13-17

> *"...Who is there to harm you if you prove zealous for what is good? But even if you should suffer for the sake of righteousness you are blessed; and do not fear their intimidation and do not become afraid and do not become intimidated by the trials but sanctify Christ as Lord in your hearts always being ready to make a defense to everyone who asks you to give account of the hope that is in you; yet with gentleness and reverence and keep a good conscious so that the thing which you are slandered, those who revile your good behavior in Christ will be put to shame; for it is better if God should*

*will it so that you suffer for doing what
it right than suffer for going wrong."*

When we walk by faith we must also commit
to endurance. Endurance removes the fear
that uncertainty can generate and places the
focus on trusting and obeying God. Here is
an illustration: There is a father who lived by
a lake that had iced over in winter. His
daughter and son wanted to go skating and
although, he thought the ice should be pretty
frozen by now, he wasn't sure. He sat the
kids on a little bench at the lake's edge. The
dad skated on the ice doing jumps and flips.
Laughing, they went and got their mother to
show her how funny daddy looked jumping
and falling all over the place. Mama sat
them down and said, "Daddy is suffering so
you won't. It is one thing for daddy's weight
to be on the ice and it not break, but it is
another for him to jump and it doesn't break.
What your daddy is doing is making sure that
when you go out there that there is no
possibility that you will sink." The mom
reassured the children since she knew how
badly they wanted to skate. She explained
that the dad was risking his life to ensure that
his children wouldn't risk theirs and possibly
die. We must remember when we trust God
in the midst of uncertainty that Jesus is the
author and the perfector of the race
(Hebrews 12:2).

The father came and got the kids pulling
them on the ice. When his daughter asked if
the ice was ok, the dad held her hand and

said that he would skate with her. They held her hands as long as she needed to feel comfortable and strong enough to skate on her own. Jesus Christ says that during the times we are weak He will sympathize with your weakness. (Hebrews 4:15; 3:14) Jesus said He is not getting off the ice because we are precious to Him. He sits continuously at the right hand of God the Father (Hebrews 8:1-2). Our trust in Christ exposes His strength in us and completes our walk of faith, rather than the weakness of our flesh.

It's All About Faith
-Chapter 6-

Hebrews 11:1-3

We are facing hard, difficult times and there is no doubt that things will get worse. The Bible says there are going to be wars, rumor of wars, deadly diseases, and we all can remember the devastation of recent hurricanes in the U.S. and the world. With so much anxiety around us, the issue becomes how will we act as we are in the midst of this turmoil? How will we act as we go through it?

Our only solution is to be productive by faith. The Tuskegee Airmen visited our church and shared stories of their lives as American fighter pilots during World War II. As they reminisced it became evident the racism they faced, including not being allowed to vote or apply for entry into the military. They said no one thought that they had the ability to fly such a complicated machine because their education stopped at the ninth grade. Each member in attendance nodded their head in agreement, recalling how much they endured in order to get a chance to fly. Can you imagine the overwhelming racism they faced? What made these men persist in the midst of adversity?

Simply put, it was their faith. It was not their ability to maneuver an airplane well, but their ability to apply their faith under extremely adverse circumstances.

Half full or half empty?

People today say the glass is half empty, while others say half full. The debate then becomes about the glass, whether it is half empty or half full. I say there is no debate, there is a glass, it has water and if you are thirsty you drink it. Then you trust God to fill it again.

In the midst of adversity, we complain about the adversity, rather than exercise the faith to walk through it. Do we come to church because it is Sunday or because God commanded us to? If we attend because God has commanded us to, then we are exercising our faith. If we attend because it is Sunday, we are relying on mama's faith and it is now a ritual.

Faith is not what I decide things to be, it is what God has determined. If I believe in things or people that have no relation to scripture, then I have useless faith. If I believe that I should play the lottery to win, then my hope is in nothing. If I believe that God is going to help me get divorced, then I don't have faith. If I believe anything that is outside the scope of God's Word, the Bible clearly sees this as having no faith at all.

As a result, many people are angry with the church. They are doing things that God has not told them to do and they get mad at God. They lash out at God, listing all the things they feel they have done for God and in return, feel shortchanged that God has not done enough for them. Yet God never told them to do these things. We have been given the Bible and it is we who choose not to read it. Instead, we rather follow anyone with a glitzy personality, preaching things that sound good. But when we follow these false prophets and our life does not change for the better, addictions are not broken, and our family is never healed, we are furious and hurt with God. Why? God has asked us for faith; faith in Him and His Word, nothing more.

We cannot make it through adversity without godly faith. If we come up with our own brand of faith, then we have a hope that is worthless. Faith, as defined in scripture, is the substance of hope.

Now faith is the substance of things hoped for, the evidence of things not seen. Hebrews 11:1, King James Version

I believe that this passage is not talking about faith as much as it is talking why one should hope. It is a passage that is often quoted but never explored to its fullest. Apostle Paul writes about faith in order to give us a real reason to hope. If I believe in something that has nothing to do with Jesus and I hope that it becomes true, Paul says that I have placed my hope falsely. My hope would not be built on the faith that God has given. This would impact all aspects of my life, including my marriage. Often couples get married and want to have a good time, all the time. But God never described marriage as non-stop fun. In fact, He said that it would give you trouble, not joy. Even to this day, newlyweds expect their marriages to mirror the Cosby show, planning to overcome their problems with laughter and love. However, if we read God's Word we would know of the trials and trouble that awaits us in marriage. The hope we have in Christ Jesus is that somewhere in the process of marriage, if we obey and follow God, He will give us joy, peace, longsuffering, gentleness, goodness, and faith.[11] It is the fruit of the Spirit that gives us the joy to make it through the marriage.

Our faith determines how we hope. If our faith is not built on a scriptural foundation, then we hope for the wrong things. As a pastor, I have been asked this question many, many times by the single ladies at the church: Why, even after praying and crying out to the Lord, have I not been blessed with a man? Why? I answered truthfully, even if they would rather not hear the truth. God never promised a man just because you read your Bible and come to church. God never

---

[11] Galatians 5.

said to come to church to meet a man or a woman. God never said that everyone would get married. So, how can we have a hope for something that God never said? We have this world view and we bring it to God and get mad when He does not produce according to the script we have written.

Apostle Paul urges us to have strong faith in adversity so that we are blessed with the answers to our hope. As the people of Israel were going through trauma and hard times, they were able to withstand because they understood the scriptures.

Hebrews 10:35 says, *"Therefore do not throw away your confidence or understanding which was great reward, for you have need of endurance."* We need to find strength and confidence because God will not stop the test. So, when you have done the will of God you can continue to hope and trust. But if you go back to the attitude you once had, you will end up back in destruction and will not receive the promise. You will not receive what you hoped for because you decided to do what you wanted.

Throughout my years as a counselor, I have seen people trip and slip up during their time of testing. For example, a single lady may consider going to the club to meet a man since no men at her church have approached her. Perhaps a husband begins to reflect on his single days with lust. When your dip low, do you still play the lottery, hoping God will understand? Our old unsaved ways can seem tempting, luring us back to old lifestyles and empty choices.

If you feel that God is not doing anything on your behalf then you will see no reason to hope. You will want to throw hope out the window. But what if you begin obeying God during your adversity? We trust the world view and not Christ, and then we blame God for not rewarding us with the blessings we seek.

It has been reported that 20% of the people that died from hardened or clogged arteries did not die as a result from cigarette smoke or some similar cause. They died from the negative outlook they adopted. They live without the hope that things can get better. It is interesting because it appears that living under this stress causes them to die from the same disease as someone who smokes a pack of cigarettes a day.

The Bible says we "turn off" hope because we have given up walking with God and have started down a path to our own destruction. God will back up and distance Himself from the person who chooses to walk away from Him during adversity.

As we continue on in Hebrews 10:39, *"But we are not of those who shrink back to destruction; but of those who have faith to preserve their souls."* We must believe that

God will keep us as we obey Him. When Peter focused on the water rather than Jesus, he sank. He went back to his "fishermen" ways of thinking and he could not continue to keep his head above the water. We must hold to the scriptures. Satan can destroy us because he tells us lies packaged as truth and we believe it. Satan tricks us into believing God is not going to do anything for you, you have been going to church and nothing has gotten better, and you have been forgotten. He says you been giving and you are still broke. In the midst of these thoughts, Satan kills our hope and spirit. Satan lets us die. We no longer want to follow or obey God. We no longer want to walk with God. We just desire to give up. However, when we give up on obeying God, we have let our hope die. Once we let our hope die we go to destruction. We keep hope alive by continuing to believe in the things that God says He is going to do.

Yet once we place our entire hope in God and His promises, we move into the realm of confident expectation. We will become soaked in the Word of God and grow in the confidence that we can accomplish our goals. As we obey God, He blesses us in the small things so that we can believe in the big things. Take the example of David and Goliath. David, a young boy, could stand in front of Goliath, the giant, after defeating the lions and the bears. It is when we keep obeying God and He keeps coming though for us that we can face the biggest issues in life and still obey Him. If we don't hold to Him in the small things, we will give up hope in the big things and we die.

Why do we keep attending church service? Some people come to church for a feeling. Others may attend hoping for things that Bible never promised. When they hear the truth, they run from church to church and like a rolling stone, gathers no moss. Instead of taking root and growing in the knowledge and love that a good church home offers, they hop to another church hoping that pastor will preach exactly what they want to hear. This is why the prophet Joel instructs us to be "hearers" **and** "doers" of the Word (James 1:22). When we expect blessings that are not promised and will not happen, we are walking in disobedience. For example, if a husband is not faithful to his wife, he does not look forward to coming home. Why? He does not want to be held accountable for his actions. When he comes home he is not welcomed because he has violated a principle of marriage. On the other hand, when a loving husband comes home, it is a blessing because he has thought of his wife throughout the day and has blessed her long before he even arrives. It is a choice to choose sin or obey God.

How can you get help with a problem if you are shutting the door on the very source of resolving it? How can the marriage become loving if a spouse continues to be unfaithful, ignoring God's tenet? We wouldn't go to the doctor and tell him to close the medical reference book. When it comes to God, we say close the book of life; I would rather rely on the world's view. This is why these Christians were giving up. In Hebrews chapter 5, Paul admonishes the people that by now they could have been teachers, instead they chose to "close the book". He continues to explain that the people have given up and become of a reprobate mind. We, just like these Christians of yesteryear, no longer have the sure hope of God's Word.

One day my son and I decided to go fishing even though I do not like fishing.

Fishing is a matter of patience. You sit holding a rod with a hook, praying that something bites. As we packed for the trip, we realized we didn't have a fishing hook. Stopping in at the local store, the clerk explained that there was different hook for bass and catfish and each needed different bait. I soon realized that he was quite knowledgeable and he quickly became a resource for me. As we sat at the edge of the lake, following all of his instructions, I still could not catch any fish. I looked across the waterfront, there was a guy catching boatloads of fish. I told my son we were going to go fish near this man and my son warned we could not go to another person's fishing hole. We stayed where we were, throwing the hook out for what seemed like infinity, and caught nothing. After three times, I was ready to go. Similarly, many of us have too little patience when waiting for God. We want results immediately, so we keep casting our lines out into the world. However, God wants us to take hold of His scriptures and meditate on them and let them soak into our souls. Although we may not see the change we hope for right away, God wants us to trust Him and His ways. Nothing is beyond the power of God's Word if we have the faith and confidence to trust in Him.

Waiting and hoping in God is an active process of obedience; it is not passive. It is in our obedience that we become approved. How many times have friends said that they are waiting for change but are just sitting in their same old situation? There are a lot of preachers that try to make this an easy process but it is not. Remember Abraham waited 25 years for the fulfillment of the promise? So, how many of us are willing to wait 25 years for our blessing? We always seem to want a quick fix. God has a long range perspective; He is focused on eternity and not on earth's time schedule. He is timeless.

We win God's approval by continuing to obey Him. Let's examine Hebrews 10:38: *"...but my righteous one shall live by faith if he shrinks back my soul has no pleasure."* "Pleasure" in this context, means to love and enjoy the person or circumstance. It also means to promote. For example, Moses was a prince but when God promoted him, he became a ruler of a nation of two million people.

Have you ever gone to work, same as you do every day, and found out you received a raise? You didn't have a clue that your name was being discussed for such a promotion. God has rewarded you because he found pleasure with you. For those of us who walk in obedience, God has given long life and the preservation of our souls. It is as if God has not only promoted his faithful, He sustains their lives daily.

We see God's awesomeness in everything we do...when we eat, drink, or pump gas. All of us breathe because there are trees. When the sun hits the leaves, the leaves will pull sap from the roots and bring it to the leaves. New York needs Central Park because of the oxygen the trees release. We don't see the sap going up the trunk to the leaves. We don't see the chemical reaction. We don't see the nitrogen and oxygen mixing together. When we walk around breathing and healthy, it is the evidence of things not seen. Through the Bible, God tells us about things that we don't see, such as:

- He tells us that He is going to come back and to have hope.

- He is telling us that He can bless us.

-   He is telling us that He can help our families live better.

-   He is telling us that He can make us more productive on our jobs.

He said even though you can't see it, you can still believe it because He said it.

We are to keep trusting and obeying Him. Living this life is all about our faith – now we must decide if it is going to be about our faith or His faith.

A Faith That Rocks
-Chapter 7-

James 2:21-26

I once applied for a job and the interviewer asked me, "Why should we hire you?" He was really asking if he were to hire me, would I make a difference in the company's bottom line. If not, then why hire me? The interviewer clearly wanted an employee that would help increase the company's productivity. Even if he were experiencing personal trouble, his concern remained steadfast; his priority was to hire the best candidate for the company.

What if God were to give you a glimpse of heaven, and allowed you one minute in His presence, then ask you how much longer would you want to live? What if God were to ask you to give Him a reason why He should keep you alive any longer? How will you answer? Will adding extra days to your life benefit His kingdom? Why should God continue to feed, clothe and keep you healthy?

God never promised that He would remove all of your life's difficulties. He allows trials, loss of loved ones, and difficult decisions to help your spiritual growth. Despite this, are we prepared to live victorious?

If your life span were extended:

- Would more people get saved and fed?

- Would more people from underserved countries receive more visits from their brothers and sisters in developed nations? Would good deeds and the gospel be taught during these visits?

- Would people in your very own community hear the Word of God taught or preached?

In short, would the kingdom of God benefit if you lived additional years? God is passionate about people passionate about His kingdom purposes. He will not change His viewpoint. So, where does that leave your faith? God desires a faith that rocks, not just the rock of faith.

A faith that rocks is a faith that makes a difference.

There are many people that believe in Jesus Christ and in the truth of His resurrection. If this is you, then you are a believer that is standing on the rock of faith. Now, consider a believer who has extraordinary faith and extraordinary vision. He is a believer that will accomplish much because his faith is on fire. This is a believer that is living a faith that rocks.

Let me explain through an example. As the original team discussed the idea of sending a satellite in space, I am sure people laughed and jeered them. However, that did not deter them and they held on to their vision. After many failed attempts, satellite technology is essential to our daily lives, providing infinite television channel options, GPS navigational assistance, and much more. Not to mention the military applications. The same could be said of the inventors of the airplane. They were most likely mocked and ridiculed as they tested their idea; however, today we fly around the world in record time. Their vision that they held on to and developed into a reality has made for a more productive world and has helped millions of people.

Each innovator started with a concept that was followed up with a belief system that they put to work. Abraham was given the promise to be a father of a nation yet he had a barren wife that remained that way for twenty five years (Romans 4:19). Yet he trusted God and became a productive individual even while waiting for the fulfillment of the promise. In the end, Abraham did in fact become the father of many nations and has been a blessing to everyone who believes.

At a time when there was no Mosaic Law, Abraham believed God for His Word (Romans 4:18-21) and demonstrates that the righteousness of God was "imputed" or given him because of his faith. It is not my understanding that Abraham was a particularly bold man, yet he went out into the wilderness, leaving all the family he knew and loved. He did this because he trusted God at His Word (Genesis 12:1-4), showing extraordinary faith. Acting on his beliefs exposed the righteousness of God, and justified Abraham by his works. James points out that in this process of obedience, God changed Abraham's life. *"You see that faith was working with his works, and as a result of the works, faith was perfected"* (James 2:22).

When God said, "I reckoned to Abraham righteousness", He is referring to "imputing" righteousness. This concept is such an important idea that we must grasp it before moving on. Impute means to deposit something in someone that they would not normally have in them. For example, it is like going to the bank and you check your balance and you now have a million dollars in your account. You know that you have not earned this money, yet you are now living off the million dollars. God sees Abraham's commitment to walk with Him and talk with Him, and has decided to put righteousness on his account. Abraham can now live righteously because the credit he was given, was given by God.

Despite the fact that Abraham lived out his faith demonstrating the imputed righteousness of God, God continually placed Abraham in situations where he had to face his fears. As Abraham and his wife traveled the land in obedience to God, they entered the territory owned by Pharaoh. Abraham was very afraid of Pharaoh and told his wife to lie and say that she is his sister (Genesis 12:10-20), in the hopes that he would not be killed. Another time, Abraham struggled with the wait God required of him to have a son (Genesis 15:1-6) causing him to make questionable decisions, such as sleeping with Hagar, a servant, in the hopes of having the promised child. Abraham was not perfect but when he was given clear directives from God, he quickly obeyed. Abraham believed God and it was "reckoned to him as righteousness." (Genesis 15:6).

Imagine the worst case scenario for Abraham? It would have to be if God were to tell him to kill his beloved son, Isaac (Genesis 22). God did just that. But Abraham, in obedience, laid his son on the altar and picked up the knife. Abraham knew it made no sense and that his heart was breaking yet decided to trust God no matter what. This powerful act of obedience and trust in God proved that he was righteous and that he would do whatever God asked, no matter the cost or sacrifice. What was Abraham thinking or even feeling? What he would tell his wife? "Hey honey, I just took your baby that you waited for twenty years and I killed him because God instructed me to do so." Imagine that! God's response to Abraham was "....*for now I know that you fear God, since you have not withheld your son, your only son, from me*" (Genesis 22:12). Did Abraham have fears, and major concerns and made some bad decisions? Yes he did, but he humbled himself and followed God's instructions when corrected. He trusted God and experienced God's power. He was not perfect but his faith rocked.

In the New Testament, Jesus Christ, at the point of salvation imputes righteousness into His people, meaning, "*When God justifies, He charges the sin of man to Christ and credits the righteousness of Christ to the believer*" (II Corinthians 5:21).[12]

"*So then as through one transgression there resulted condemnation to all men, even so through one act of righteousness there resulted justification of life to all men.*"

Romans 5:18

It does not matter what we face in this life; all that matters who we place our faith in – Christ and Christ alone (John 12:23-26).

---

[12] Nelson's Illustrated Bible Dictionary, Copyright © 1986, Thomas Nelson Publishers.

Like Abraham, a believer can demonstrate the powerful work of God in his life by trusting God for His Word applying it each and every day. They can now apply themselves to the task at hand and complete it in victory. These believers are then walking in the truth that God has placed in them. They show themselves to be as God created them and as His Word describes.

Armed with this understanding, you can now walk in these scriptures:

- *"But in all these things we overwhelmingly conquer through Him who loved us."* (Romans 8:37)

- *"I can do all things through Him who strengthens me."* (Philippians 4:13)

You, as well as every believer, can experience a faith that rocks.

A faith that rocks kind of marriage...

As adults, when your marriage is rocky and at times, you find that you don't like (notice, I said like) your spouse anymore and habits you once thought adorable now have become irritants...do you have a faith that rocks?

Sometimes in a marriage, you may think that if you remain faithful and steadfast that your spouse may view it as a weakness and try to take advantage of you. Are you willing to believe God at His Word and obey Him daily? What if your spouse has gotten sick or the illness has continued for a long time, will you show a faith that rocks? What would you do? Can you consistently obey God in your marriage when nothing seems to change for the better? Will you be obedient to God even as fear start to creep up in your mind? Perhaps you are single and your biological clock keeps on ticking and you are afraid that God desires a single life for you and it is not your desire. Would you willingly submit to the Lord and keep working for Him, serving Him and trusting Him each day? Or would your fears lead you to make decisions that do not please God? The answer to these questions reveals if you have a faith that rocks.

A person who is living a faith that rocks is not going to talk, walk or act the same. Changes start to take place in their minds and hearts. Perhaps they begin to lose the desire for drinking beer and partying. Perhaps the lure of a promiscuous lifestyle holds less of an appeal. They are no longer focused on impressing others. An inward change begins when we apply ourselves to the Word of God (Romans 12:2; II Corinthians 3:18). This means that the character of Christ, provided as a result of the transformation when we were saved (II Corinthians 5:17), manifest itself in the believers' day-to-day life demonstrating that the believer stands "justified" before God (Hebrews 10:14).

Christ provided the ultimate example of a faith that rocks when He went to Calvary's Cross for us (1 Peter 2:21-25). It did not matter how difficult things became for Christ (Hebrews 12:2-3), He had to be about His Father's business. He said it did not matter what the enemy tried to do to Him. Christ remained focused and told Peter "to get behind me Satan", when he doubted (Matthew 16:23). The person who follows this example is a person whose character is so adjusted to the disposition of Jesus Christ that this person's faith will rock. This character exposes the righteousness of God that was imputed into the believer at the point of salvation. "The cross of Jesus is a public demonstration of God's righteousness. God accounts or transfers the righteousness of Christ to those who trust in Him (Romans 4:3-22; Galatians 3:6; Philippians 3:9). We do not become righteous because of our inherent goodness; God sees us as righteous because of our identification by faith with His Son."[13] We do have to commit to abide in God's Word (John 15:1-11) and work out this salvation in fear and trembling (Philippians 2:12-13) as God accomplish His purposes for our lives.

Jesus, on earth, changed the world. The person who best imitates this life of obedience is Paul. Even as Paul would

---

[13] Nelson's Illustrated Bible Dictionary, Copyright © 1986, Thomas Nelson Publishers.

experience the worse beatings of his life, he would say that the sufferings of this present time cannot compare to the glory that is to be revealed (Romans 8:18). Paul was thrown in jail yet he used this time to witness to the soldiers about Jesus Christ. Paul decided to write four different books in prison in order to continue the ministry of God: Ephesians, Philippians, Colossians and Philemon. Paul chose to rejoice because he learned to be content in whatever state he was in, God's standards dominated his life (Philippians 4:10-14) and he increasingly took on the character of Jesus Christ (Galatians 2:21; Philippians 4:9). Paul's commitment to fulfill the calling on his life caused problems for the disciples at first (Acts 15), but through his unwavering commitment, millions of people all around the world can be taught the gospel. What a transformation for a person who once killed Christians. Look at how the commitment to apply himself to God's call on his life made a difference.

The challenge...

Paul's faith rocked so much that it continues to rock us today. We are often surrounded by people who talk "about" the Bible everyday but there is no evidence of change in their homes or in their lives. Today, people follow Christ not for who He is but rather the benefits He provides.

When are you going to decide to get involved and become an excellent example for other believers? When are you going to take all of the knowledge and information that God has blessed you with and leave a legacy wherever God plants you? When do you walk in the fullness of what God has declared you to be? (Ephesians 4:13; Colossians 2:9-10)

This is the reason God has called the just to live by faith (Habakkuk 2:4). The faithful are not looking for tomorrow to activate their faith, rather, they are committed to obeying God now, regardless of the tension, fear or difficulty. Living by faith means, even if the issue or problem has not gone away, the individual is most concerned about obeying Him **now**. In Matthew 25, when the righteous come before Him, they said we cannot remember feeding the poor, clothing the naked or dealing with those in prison. He said when you did it to the least of them they did it unto Him. Every time a believer looks beyond his or her personal struggles and commits an act of love and kindness, then they have made a difference.

In the midst of difficult times, you are to let the scriptures dominate how you act and think. In the hard times of life, trust God to bring you through. This process leads to God's perfecting work in the life of the believer. It is this perfecting process that allows a believer to make it through the most difficult issues they may experience (2 Peter 1:3-11). *"For he who lacks these qualities is blind or short-sighted, having forgotten his purification from his former sins. Therefore, brethren, be all the more diligent to make certain about His calling and choosing you; for as long as you practice these things, you will never stumble; for in this way the entrance into the eternal kingdom of our Lord and Savior Jesus Christ will be abundantly supplied to you*" (2 Peter 1:9-11; NASU).

This is the power of the perfecting process and it is this that cancels fear. *"But whoever keeps His Word, in him the love of God has truly been perfected. By this we know that we are in Him"* (I John 2:5; NASU). *"There is no fear in love; but, perfect love cast out fear, because fear involves punishment, and the one who hears is not perfected in love"* (I John 5:18).

James address this perfecting work of God when he says; *"You see that faith was working with his works, and as a result of the works, faith was perfected."* (James 2:22; NASU)

Abraham showed imperfection when he would lie and sin. He was no perfect man yet God perfected him because he was committed to do what God told him to do - no matter what. This belief in God caused Abraham's change. We are offered the same challenge as believers.

The word "perfect" does not refer to perfect people or a perfect person. If there was a perfect person then I John1:10 is untrue:

"...if a man says he has no sin he is a liar and the truth is not in him". But believers will transition to the point where the word means "finished or complete". Abraham had come to a point in his life where there was nothing else that God needed to do. When Abraham was willing to sacrifice his son he waited for twenty five years, while still trusting God to produce a great nation illustrated his complete trust in God. God's work to establish Abraham's faith was finished.

When are we, who are in Christ, going to graduate to a higher level of trust? Many times, God is saying I have a better place for you and a better plan than you have for yourself. If we start living and believing like Abraham, we will be able to take on all the trials, heartaches and difficulties and still live a productive glorious life. If the only thing we do is want more knowledge and never act on it, then all is wasted. *"Now concerning things sacrificed to idols, we know that we all have knowledge. Knowledge makes arrogant, but love edifies. If anyone supposes that he knows anything, he has not yet known as he ought to know; but if anyone loves God, he is known by Him"* (1 Corinthians 8:1-3; NASU). *"But are you willing to recognize, you foolish fellow, that faith without works is useless?"* (James 2:20; NASU)

He says just *"as the body without the spirit is dead so also faith without works is dead"* (James 2:26; NIV). "Dead" means that it is useless. The Bible says faith creates an excitement because when it is attached to works God blesses. *"And He said to them, "Because of the littleness of your faith; for truly I say to you, if you have faith the size of a mustard seed, you will say to this mountain, 'Move from here to there,' and it will move; and nothing will be impossible to you. But this kind does not go out except by prayer and fasting"* (Matt 17:20-21; NASU).

Faith makes you appreciate Jesus Christ

Faith is experiencing Him and knowing Him, which makes you want to serve Him. Many times I look back into the scriptures and I see people like Ruth, her faith rocked. She said that she believed in the God that Naomi believed in and she was willing to die wherever Naomi was going to die. Ruth told Naomi she was going to become her family when everyone else had died or left her. She told Naomi that she was not going to let her die and she said; 'I am going back with you.' Ruth would go out and do whatever it takes to support Naomi; she would even become a slave. Because of her faithfulness, Jesus came from her line and so her faith is still rocking today. I look at Esther and she was not much of a God sent believer. She was a concubine that decided to save a nation when Mordecai came to her. She decided to risk her life and believe that God was going to make the difference. If it was not for Esther, the Jews in Babylon would have been destroyed. One woman's faith rocked.

Today we want God to be our "sugar daddy". We say, 'God I want peace and joy, and please just drop it in my lap. I don't want to grow and have the fruit of the spirit". Or perhaps, we say, "I need a car God...could you just bring it to me?" If He gave us all that we ask, what would we do with it? God is willing to provide us the desires of our hearts but we must first abide in Him, no matter the struggles or the fears within (John 15:1-10). We do not need faith that is a rock but faith that rocks.

God puts in your life what will always take you higher and higher. Through this process, as God is perfecting us, He will take us to higher levels that will stretch and teach us to trust in Him. God is infinite and there is no plateau to arrive at with God. It is always higher and higher. As such, a person that has faith is a person that must **walk** in faith. I don't like the word "mature" to describe a Christian. When a person thinks they are mature they think that they have arrived. "Mature" means I am complete and when there is a problem, I know what needs to be done; I know where to go and how to fix it. Anyone who thinks they have arrived has an inflated vision of themselves. Anytime I think that I have arrived as a pastor, I am sure to falter because there is no way I can say I have "arrived" in comparison to God, **meaning we will never come to a point in our faith where we know everything**. If we are not walking by faith then we don't trigger the righteousness that He has imputed and as a result we fall short. It is this faith that glues us to God and perfects us so that our experience of God becomes as Paul describes; *"I have been crucified with Christ; and it is no longer I who live, but Christ lives in me; and the life which I now live in the flesh I live by faith in the Son of God"* (Galatians 2:20). He died *'to give us life and life abundantly'* (John 10:10; NASU). He also died so that we can have a friendship with Him (John 15:13-15).

The process explained in this chapter causes our prayers to rock. James 5:16 teaches, *"The effective prayer of a righteous man can accomplish much"* (NASU). Also, the Lord promises to grant us what we wish if we abide in Him.[14] So the Word says our prayers can avail much.[15] When we demonstrate our faith by our works, we abide in Christ. Our abiding bears much fruit which exposes the imputed righteousness of God. This righteousness allows our prayers to accomplish much. As a result our life is very productive because the life in us dominates how we think and act (Colossians 3:1-4). When you have this kind of faith, your life rocks because God promises are fulfilled (Romans 4:18-21). He will answer our prayers because we demonstrate the righteousness that He has imputed. "The

---

[14] John 15:7.

[15] James 5:16.

effective fervent prayer of a righteous man avails much" (James 5:16).

This passage highlights a call to action that preserves a believer's soul and makes him productive in difficult situations:

"But remember the former days, when, after being enlightened, you endured a great conflict of sufferings, partly by being made a public spectacle through reproaches and tribulations, and partly by becoming sharers with those who were so treated. For you showed sympathy to the prisoners and accepted joyfully the seizure of your property, knowing that you have for yourselves a better possession and a lasting one. Therefore, do not throw away your confidence, which has a great reward. For you have need of endurance, so that when you have done the will of God, you may receive what was promised.

FOR YET IN A VERY LITTLE WHILE, HE WHO IS COMING WILL COME, AND WILL NOT DELAY. BUT MY RIGHTEOUS ONE SHALL LIVE BY FAITH;
AND IF HE SHRINKS BACK, MY SOUL HAS NO PLEASURE IN HIM.

But we are not of those who shrink back to destruction, but of those who have faith to the preserving of the soul."

(Hebrews 10:32-39; NASU *my emphasis added*)

Also,

> *For whatever is born of God overcomes the world; and this is the victory that has overcome the world – our faith.* (I John 5:4: NASU)

No need to fear when faith is demonstrated by our works. It stimulates the righteous development of our character, due to righteousness that is imputed, and this character of Christ leads to our perfecting (I John 2:5). This perfecting casts out fear. We achieve the purpose of Christ death and that is to provide us 'life and life abundantly' (John 10:10) and a friendship with God (John 15:1-17).

"What then shall we say to these things? If God is for us, who is against us?" (Romans 8:31; NASU)

"But in all these things we overwhelmingly conquer through Him who loved us" (Romans 8:37; NASU).

This is a faith that rocks and preserves the soul.

No matter how impossible something may seem, if the Word of God directs believers, we must trust God and obey. Just like it was for inventors of planes or satellites, believers of Christ will withstand the ridicule of the world and live by faith. In fact, our lives will impact many people for the glory of God, giving us purpose and meaning. It is this life that blesses the believer as well as those around them. This usefulness and powerful experiences blesses God.

GIVE FEAR A KNOCK OUT PUNCH
BIBLICAL STRATEGIES TO TEACH YOU TO
OVERCOME EVERY FEAR THAT BINDS YOU.

ABOUT THE AUTHOR

Dr. Paul Cannings, long considered "the teacher's teacher" among leading pastor and clergy, is the Senior Pastor of Living Word Fellowship Church in Houston, Texas. He provides spiritual direction and leadership to a growing congregation and is a sought after speaker on the national and international stage.

Dr. Cannings is also the President of Living Word Christian Academy, a Christian school for children from 2 years old – 8th grade. Striving to better the community, he also founded the area's only four-star accredited pre-school. He has also established an outreach ministry; The Christian Outreach Center, to help families living in crisis.

He can be heard locally in Houston on KHCB (khcb.org)/105.7 fm, where he serves as a bible study leader on "The Pastor's Corner" and is the host of a live question and answer program called "The Pastor's Study". He is also a adjunct professor at the College of Biblical Studies.

He is the author of numerous books, including *Why Can't Mondays Be More Like Sundays?* and *Biblical Answers for the 21st Century Church*, a resource for church leaders tackling today's toughest questions.

EDUCATION
Skyline High School
Dallas, TX (1973-1975)

B.A.-Austin College
Sherman, TX (1975-1979)
Honors: Outstanding Service
Award as Chairman of the Student
Development Board, All Conference
& All District Award in Soccer

Th.M.- Bible & Christian Education
Dallas Theological Seminary
Seminary 1981-1985

PhD.- Theological Studies
Religion & Society
Oxford Graduate School
Dayton, Tenn. (1991)
(some course work at Oxford University)

Visit our online resource center at
www.powerwalkministries.org

Listen to our radio broadcast live at
www.oneplace.com/ministries/power_walk

View our streaming videos at
www.streamingfaith.com
www.paulcannings.tv
http://www.youtube.com/powerwalk

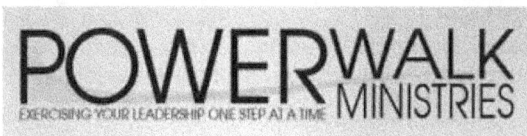

POWERWALK MINISTRIES
EXERCISING YOUR LEADERSHIP ONE STEP AT A TIME

www.ingramcontent.com/pod-product-compliance
Lightning Source LLC
Chambersburg PA
CBHW051835040426
42447CB00006B/545